DISCARD

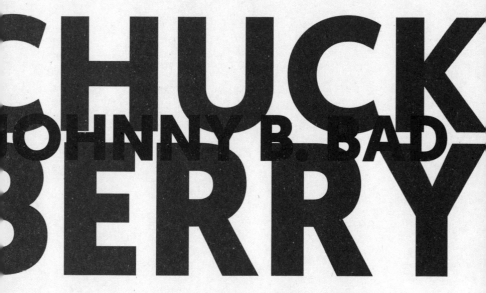

CHUCK BERRY

JOHNNY B. BAD

The Making of **HAIL! HAIL! ROCK AND ROLL**

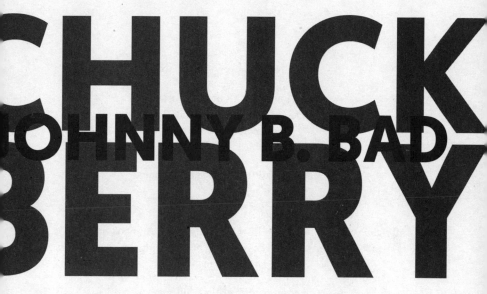

CHUCK
JOHNNY B. BAD
BERRY

The Making of **HAIL! HAIL! ROCK AND ROLL**

tephanie Bennett

with Thomas D. Adelman

A Vireo Book, Rare Bird Book
Los Angeles, Calif.

Publisher's Cataloging-in-Publication Data
Names: Bennett, Stephanie, author.
Title: Johnny B Bad: The Making of the Movie Chuck Berry Hail! Hail!
Rock 'N' Roll / Stephanie Bennett.
Description: First Hardcover Original Edition | A Genuine Vireo Book |
New York; NY; Los Angeles, CA: Rare Bird Books, 2019.
Identifiers: ISBN 9781947856905
Subjects: LCSH Berry, Chuck. | Chuck Berry Hail! Hail! Rock 'N' Roll
(Motion picture) | Documentary films—United States—History and
criticism. | Musicians in motion pictures. | Concert films—History and
criticism. | Rock films—History and criticism. |
BISAC PERFORMING ARTS / Film / Genres / Documentary |
PERFORMING ARTS / Film / History & Criticism
Classification: LCC PN1995.9.D6 .B3855 2019 | DDC 780.26/7—dc23

To Jane Rose, Suzie Petersen, and Jane Ayer.
For whose courage and support, I will be forever grateful.

FEATURED PLAYERS

Stephanie Bennett	Producer
Taylor Hackford	Director
Thomas D. Adelman	Line Producer
Keith Richards	Musical Director
Robbie Robertson	Creative Consultant
Helen Mirren	Actress
Albert Spevak	Business Affairs
Jim Mervis	Producer's Partner
Dick Allen	Chuck Berry's Former Tour Manager
Jane Ayer	Publicity for Universal Pictures
Jane Rose	Keith Richards' Manager
Michael Frondelli	Audio Engineer
Oliver Stapleton	Cinematographer
Suzie Petersen	Head of MCA/Universal
Chuck Berry	Artist
Johnnie Johnson	Artist
Steve Jordan	Artist
Joey Spampinato	Artist
Robert Cray	Artist
Bo Diddley	Artist
Little Richard	Artist
Bruce Springsteen	Artist

CONTENTS

FOREWORD
by Taylor Hackford

I N 1985, I WAS finishing postproduction on my dance film
White Nights, starring Mikhail Baryshnikov and Gregory
Hines, when I got a call from an English producer, Stephanie
Bennett, asking if I'd be interested in making a documentary
to commemorate Chuck Berry's sixtieth birthday. Being
a child of rock 'n' roll who'd experienced the blossoming of
this All-American artform in the fifties and sixties, this was
an opportunity I had to take seriously—there was no one like
Chuck Berry—he was the gold standard—the greatest singer,
songwriter, and guitarist of his generation.

I met with Stephanie and found her to be an interesting
blend of middle-class English professionalism and "ducker
and diver" entrepreneurship. In addition to having produced
docs on The Everly Brothers and The Beach Boys, she had
accomplished the seemingly impossible task of securing
the rights to *The Compleat Beatles*, one of the first and best
documentaries on The Beatles. I asked her what commitments
she already had in place, and she said that Universal Home
Video was interested in financing a star-studded concert film
featuring major rock 'n' roll artists who had been influenced
by Chuck's songs and musical style. Basically, that included
everyone in rock 'n' roll. The only artist she'd already locked-
up was Keith Richards, as musical director of this concert.
Being a Rolling Stones fan, this pleased me immensely,
because I knew there would be a high musical quotient to

any concert Keith was involved in—plus he'd always made it known that his number-one influence was Chuck Berry. Then I asked the most important question: "Was Chuck onboard." Stephanie blinked: "Chuck says he's in if the price is right, and Universal is ready to pay him handsomely for his musical and personal rights." Of course, I knew what that meant: Stephanie and whoever joined her as director were in for a bumpy ride. I was familiar with the myriad stories about Chuck's "bad boy" persona—he'd already served three stints in prison (for grand-theft auto, sex-trafficking, and tax evasion), and was notorious for demanding cash up-front before he'd play a gig—often changing the terms in the process. However, instead of these warning signs deterring me, they were major attractions because I knew that any film featuring Chuck Berry could not be boring. (One problem I have with celebratory documentaries is that they are too often "gooey valentines," glossing over the personality flaws that often go hand in glove with an artist's ascent to fame and fortune.) With Chuck Berry, I knew it would be impossible to hide his dark underside— the camera doesn't lie, so if I could capture him candidly in action—I was sure I'd make a provocative film. Little did I know how accurate my prediction would turn out to be.

I told Stephanie what I'd need to direct this film: total artistic control, including final cut. She immediately agreed. I also said that I was not interested in simply making a concert film—I wanted to capture a candid portrait of Chuck as he interreacted with all the guest artists he'd be rehearsing with before the concert, *and also* I wanted Chuck to agree to speak with me on-camera about his complicated career. Stephanie liked my concepts and said that she'd get Universal to approve my deal points. However, as for Chuck agreeing to speak with me on-camera, I would have to convince him myself—Chuck was the executive producer of the film.

The first step in putting this project together was for all of us to meet with Chuck to make sure we were all on the same page, so Stephanie, her line producer, Thomas Adelman, Keith, and I flew to Chicago where he was performing at the Chicago Blues Festival. This experience turned out to be prescient in defining the anarchic nature of what this project would become. We met Chuck backstage at the festival, before he was about to go onstage. Being a hustling producer, Stephanie had encouraged the promoter to have photographers present to capture Keith and Chuck together—hoping this would encourage both men to commit publicly to our film. It was interesting to watch Stephanie work—she boldly suggested to the promoter that he invite Keith on stage at the end of Chuck's set for an impromptu jam. Chuck eyed Stephanie coldly, but he didn't object, nodding his approval. At the end of Chuck's set, Keith walked out on stage, and the audience went insane, giving the Rolling Stone an ovation that dwarfed what they had given Chuck earlier. I watched Chuck's reaction, ever the showman he welcomed Keith with open arms, but I also detected a veiled resentment—a clear slap in the face that this second generation rock 'n' roller was a much bigger star than he was. Keith righteously put the audience in their place: "I stole every lick this man ever created, he's the best ever." (Later, Keith told me that the last time they'd met, Chuck had punched him in the face, mistaking him for a troublesome fan. While Keith was good-natured about this insult, I could tell he was still sensitive about the incident. At that moment, I saw what the theme of this film should be: creator versus pupil. Keith, the pupil, who had risen to greater heights of fame and fortune than his mentor, Chuck, who had actually invented the art form.

After the concert we had planned to sit down in the restaurant at our hotel to discuss the film, but Chuck insisted that we have the meeting in his Winnebago, a huge motor home he'd driven up from his home in St Louis. When Stephanie tried to protest, suggesting that we take a limo, Chuck laid down the law: "Nobody drives Chuck Berry, but Chuck Berry." Instead of sitting down to a quiet meal, he pulled his giant rig into a MacDonalds for take-out burgers and shakes. We ate as he drove us around his old Chicago haunts: past Chess Records on Michigan Ave where he literally turned the wrong direction onto this major Chicago thoroughfare, blowing his air horn to warn six lanes of on-coming traffic to get out of his way. Chuck was serving notice: "You are all in for one wild ride." Forewarned, none of us backed down.

Personally, I was thrilled, Chuck was more quirky, charming, and human than I'd ever imagined. I knew he'd be a fantastic on-camera personality—my movie star. I told him honestly that I was not there to do a hatch-job/expose on his life, but neither was I interested in doing a puff piece. I saw this film as an opportunity of creating a lasting legacy of his career, and I wanted him to speak with me candidly about his life and music. To my delight, he agreed "to let me in." We cemented our relationship with a handshake. Of course, anyone who'd worked with Chuck Berry over the years knew that his commitments and handshakes were malleable, but I was a novice and had to discover his mercurial style for myself.

We recruited an incredibly talented group of artists, both in front of and behind the camera, who had all come to celebrate the brilliance of this man who had indelibly influenced our lives. But to our amazement, Chuck seemed to sabotage our efforts at every turn, refusing to appear on the first day of shooting until he was paid an extra $25,000 in cash, delivered in a brown paper bag. When he finally appeared seven hours later, he was totally charming and cooperative. (He pulled me aside conspiratorially and said: "Taylor, this has nothing to do with you and me, it's just business.") Actually, I normally produce and direct my films, but in this instance I was happy that I did not take producer credit, it was up to Stephanie and Associate Producer Albert Spevak to satisfy Chuck's avaricious demands each day, which allowed me to work with him on purely creative issues. I'm sure it preserved our relationship. Still, he could be totally exasperating creatively. On the second day of shooting, he told me he wouldn't be available on Wednesday: "I've got a gig at the Ohio State Fair." Shocked, I protested: "Chuck I've only got six days to shoot this entire film, including the concert! I need every minute of shooting-time to make it work." Unfortunately, my dramatics didn't faze Chuck: "I've got a contract in Ohio, they're paying me twenty-five grand and I'm going". (In reality, he was being paid more by Universal than anyone on the film—$500,000— but he seemed to have a psychotic need "to put one over" on the production every day. It was exhausting.) I responded to his bombshell by saying that I would follow him to Ohio with a small film crew. His response was typical: "Fine with me, but I ain't payin'." The resulting sequence turned out to be one of the best in the film: Bruce Springsteen narrated it, recalling his experience backing up Chuck on the road when he and the E-Street Band were nobodies.

Without a doubt Chuck was the most difficult, unpredictable, and temperamental "movie star" I've ever worked with, but my philosophy is: When you're working with a genius, you can't expect them to be "normal." Chuck's unpredictability and his sly charm were what made him irresistible on screen, so as a filmmaker I had a ball making *Hail! Hail!*. The fact that I had a costar as strong, talented, and experienced as Keith Richards was my ace in the hole. Chuck was absolutely diabolical in his treatment of Keith— complimentary one moment and cruelly punishing the next. Most spoiled rock 'n' roll stars would have walked out early in the process, but Keith was there for one reason—to celebrate his mentor in front of the world—and no amount of shit from Chuck could dissuade him. I grew to have immense respect for Keith Richards.

This book by Stephanie Bennett and Thomas Adelman will probably tell a different story—they didn't "enjoy" the filmmaking process—they had to do the dirty work. Stephanie told me about the verbal abuse and sexual harassment she and Jane Rose, Keith's manager, had to put up with. None of this abusive behavior happened in front of me, but I didn't doubt it. Chuck dished out his humiliating abuse to all of us in one form or another. Both Stephanie and Jane were tough professionals who knew the world of rock 'n' roll—they would have hollered if they felt truly threatened, but like the rest of us professionals, these women took the "heat" to get the film made.

Trying to understand Chuck Berry is probably impossible. The first generation of rock 'n' roll was populated by rough, working-class men who literally had to fight to be heard. In 1955, Chuck was carrying three jobs to feed his family, and only played his music on weekends in East St Louis, Illinois— one of the toughest neighborhoods in the US. But Chuck Berry had ambition, literary ambition, that he secretly fostered. In the bonus materials I included for the *Hail! Hail!* DVD, Robbie Robertson has a conversation with Chuck in which Chuck spontaneously starts reciting English poetry that he learned in prison when he was eighteen years of age. He could still recite all that iambic pentameter by heart. To me that moment revealed the huge world of white culture and intellectualism that Chuck craved in his heart but had no way of accessing. It was like a big "keep out" sign, saying "uneducated blacks need not apply," against which he was hurling himself. That combined with a sexual fantasy about white women that he was honest about in his biography, made up the reality that Stephanie and Jane and the rest of us had to deal with.

Still, with all of his diabolical behavior, I loved Chuck Berry. As much as he tried to hide, he did keep his word to me, he "let me in" and I believe that a substantial portion of this great artist's personality, his incredible energy, and his dark tortured soul was captured forever in *Hail! Hail! Rock 'N' Roll*.

INTRODUCTION

By Stephanie Bennett

O N MARCH 18, 2017, Chuck Berry died and the phone calls and emails started coming in. I was the producer of the film *Hail! Hail! Rock 'N' Roll*. People asked me, "How do you feel?"

It's a tough question to answer in one sentence.

I have produced many films with famous musical stars including: "The Compleat Beatles," which was the first music documentary on home video, films about Joni Mitchell, Roy Orbison's " Black and White Night," the Everly Brothers, and the Beach Boys, among others.

I was always respectful of the artists and their art and I would say, in all cases, everyone was happy with the end result. Making a film about the legend Chuck Berry seemed like a feather in my cap as producer.

Taylor Hackford agreed to be the director, Keith Richards agreed to be the musical director, and I thought Chuck Berry would have been thrilled. But he wasn't. Chuck was a very private person; he rarely ever did interviews, or agreed to be filmed, and suddenly we were on his doorstep. Literally we brought crews and cameramen into his home in Wentzville, Missouri, and took him out of his comfort zone, whether it was going to Keith Richard's house in Jamaica or meeting up in Chicago. It would ultimately take two years to make the film and during that time we would have the most intimate close-up look at Chuck Berry. It is not always a pretty picture.

Taylor Hackford, the director, described working with Chuck as more difficult than working with any movie star. "We all came to Berry Park expecting to celebrate this incredible genius. What we found was a very conflicted genius who gave us a lot of trouble. The scorpion stung us with his stinger."

As Keith Richards says about the film, "Chuck opened the door and he thought he could just let a few people in, but goddamn it, the world came in. He thought he could control it when they came in, but the outside world flooded in and maybe that's what's so intriguing. The more you found out about him, the less you knew."

Helen Mirren, who was there for much of our journey and filming, remembered, "Chuck was very charismatic. What touched me about him was he seemed sweet yet he was a monster. He was an unbelievably wild man." We would all see the different sides of this complex and fascinating person. No one could dispute that he was the godfather of rock and roll. It was our intention to show the world a great artist, to make a film Chuck would be proud of, and to showcase his talent while exploring his personal life.

As the project progressed, his lack of cooperation would make it difficult. This book tries to explore some of the reasons for this—was it about money, was it about control? We know growing up in the South he faced discrimination because of his color, and his time in jail would change him forever. Johnnie Johnson said, "he wasn't much different to me." But I could see how he acted with other people, and I knew he had a chip on his shoulder. He was angry as to how the law had treated him and thought everyone wanted to cheat him. He was definitely a different person after he came out of prison.

Did he trust anyone? Could he trust us? His inflexibility would be costly to the film in time and money. Leading up to this oral history is a chapter of excerpts from the interviews Taylor filmed with Chuck, Robbie Robertson, Little Richard, Bo Diddley, and Dick Allen, who was Chuck's booking agent. They provide an insight into his past and perhaps shed some light on Chuck's behavior during production. Tom Adelman, Taylor Hackford, Keith Richards, and Jane Rose (Keith's manager), and I would travel with Chuck to Chicago, to his home, Berry Park in Wentzville, Missouri, where we stayed for one night and then to Keith's house in Jamaica before the cameras would roll.

During these trips, we got to interact with Chuck close up. His actions during production over a period of two years gave us a perspective that most people would never get to see.

So it was initially an honor to be able to make a film about Chuck Berry, arguably the most important figure in rock and roll history. I was flattered he chose me as his producer but later came to realize he thought I was part of the deal and if he couldn't have me then he would get as much money as he possibly could. I had to keep the film on track and protect especially Taylor and Keith from Chuck's behavior and constant demands. Our executive at Universal, Suzie Peterson, would say "it was horrendous. I was afraid for my job," as we constantly went back to them for more money. Ultimately I think they, Universal, and we felt the show must go on. I worked with Chuck on the film *Hail! Hail! Rock 'N' Roll*, including preproduction, production, and promotion. This book is about my life with Chuck during that time and contains my recollections along with the thoughts and stories of many others who worked on the film. It is also a film about Chuck and Keith's relationship. As Keith said, "I mean everybody said

I'm mad to take on the gig. So I ordered the straight jacket, allow six to eight weeks for delivery, and if anybody was going to do it, I wanted it to be me."

This book could not have happened without Tom Adelman who, with me, interviewed over fifteen people and contributed his own recollections. Everyone has a story. This oral history provides a close-up picture of a complicated genius and a reluctant star. We would succeed in making the film in spite of that star, Chuck Berry, because we knew it would be a classic rock and roll film and the most intimate picture of the man that anyone would probably ever see.

In the film the director Taylor Hackford asked Chuck, "how do you want to be remembered?" and Chuck replied: "I just hope they'll tell the truth, pro or con."

CHAPTER ONE

A Conversation with Chuck Berry and Robbie Robertson

A CONVERSATION WITH CHUCK Berry and Robbie Robertson and a historical round-robin conversation with Chuck Berry, Bo Diddley and Little Richard. Our book opens with, and we thought appropriately so, two chapters from the DVD of Hail! Hail! Rock 'N' Roll, *which give some background on Chuck Berry. In chapter one, Robbie Robertson, formerly of The Band, sat down with Chuck. While going through some of his scrapbooks, he got Chuck to open up a bit about his early career and this was truly a rare occasion where Chuck talked unfiltered about his life. The second chapter is an interview that director Taylor Hackford did with Chuck Berry, Little Richard, and Bo Diddley where they talk about being on the road in the early days of the fifties. This chapter includes a few comments from Johnny Johnson and Carl Perkins to add some perspective on Chuck Berry in his early days. Both these sections are unique, for it is rare to get three legends like this together and also to hear Chuck talk about his music. These chapters give some insight into what motivated these artists in their world as they dealt with touring and racism.*

CHUCK BERRY/ROBBIE ROBERTSON INTERVIEW

TAYLOR HACKFORD: A great musician who is not in the movie is Robbie Robertson. Robbie was the creative consultant on the film. He is a friend of mine and gave us a great deal of input and insight during the making of the film. He wasn't onstage in St. Louis; however, after the concert, he got together with Chuck at his house in Hollywood, the only circular acre lot in all of Los Angeles, as Chuck described it, and they went through Chuck's scrapbook. An interesting thing happened. Robbie, by being a consummate guitarist/musician, was able to put Chuck immediately at ease. There was a respect and comradery there. Secondly, going through the scrapbook, it allowed Chuck to get nostalgic with a look at his past, and I think he discovered certain things, even though we covered a lot in the film, and got a real taste of a different Chuck Berry with Robbie Robertson.

ROBBIE ROBERTSON: Who is this? (Looking at a photo of Chuck Berry.)

CHUCK BERRY: That's the guy that they call the father of rock and roll. Chuck Berry.

RR: I guess I was maybe twelve years old when I first saw this, but when I first heard this, for me there was a kind of separation in your version of rock and roll and everybody else's. It was like "where did this guy ever hear of Beethoven and Tchaikovsky," the lyrics you were using. It seemed like there was such a sophistication in it. It wasn't be bop a loo la and wop bop a loo ma. It was the lyrics going by, like bang, flying by. It wasn't just somebody trying to get to the end of the song, it was somebody who was actually, each line was written out.

CB: Trying to tell a story, Robbie. It came from actually poetry. Poetry portrays a scene or a story, and that's the way my lyrics were originally from some thought, from it came a story and then proceeded with a music or some riff that reminded me of some situation that brought about a story. It didn't come from music, it come from lyrics.

RR: The poetry. You knew about poetry. You were into poetry.

CB: Very much so, very much so.

RR: But that's kind of unusual in the period, that rebel period and everything. I mean poetry and sissy kind of went together, so it was a rebel against a rebel.

CB: I don't know. Beatniks were into poetry a lot.

RR: That's true.

CB: (Looking at a picture.) Maybe I was nineteen. Young and tender…right there you can see I began to learn things.

RR: Yeah, the innocence is slipping away.

CB: I began to lose money then.

RR: How come this is burnt.

CB: Fran started the scrapbook in '57. We had a fire at the office in I think '70 and it burned our scrapbook, and these are the survivals. And what we have here is my first car that my sister signed for. The first one was a Ford, the second one was a Plymouth…'33 an '34. And that is a library card. And, ah, check stuff from National Tea company. And check stubs. I'm in the money here. I'm making ninety dollars a week here at Fisher Body Auto.

RR: What were you doing there?

CB: Ah, sweeping floors. I was singing…

RR: This Musician Union card here.

CB: Oh, I got that in '54. Started earning…

RR: But who's this person's name on here.

CB: Oh, that's my name. I sort of camouflaged that "N"...Chuck Barron, because I wasn't big and my daddy was a deacon.

RR: He didn't want you playing this music, huh?

CB: That's for sure. And the American Car Foundry. See, I worked.

RR: You paid your dues.

CB: At twenty-one dollars a night to play music you have to have another job. This is me here in the Baptist Church choir. We all look alike there.

RR: No, no. All of them but you.

CB: Okay, and that's in the Baptist Church choir, and that's my eighth grade graduation. And I don't know why they always put me in the top row. I majored in math. I flunked all my history.

RR: This is you playing the saxophone. That's Chuck Berry playing the saxophone, believe it or not.

CB: Well Johnnie Johnson inspired me to do that.

RR: Old bullet-hand Johnnie.

CB: He had a hair hammer right hand on treble and a dynamite left base boogie-woogie. This here is also the Cosmo here. This was a going away party when "Maybelline" hit. This was about September of 1955, and I left the city on August 15, 1955, to go to Gleason's Bar, which is here. Gleason's Bar. It says August 15, 1955. Cleveland, Ohio, $800 a week. Behind twenty-one dollars a night at the Cosmo Club over there. Sixty dollars with the whole band at the Green Dragon but Gleason's paid $800 a week.

RR: That's when you decided, I think this is for me.

CB: Yeah, this is the way to go. And, of course, you know who this guy is. Robbie, this is Muddy Waters band, and this is a disc jockey in Chicago. He was pretty big named Al somebody. But this is Leonard Chess in his glory, with a hitmaker on his hands. And this was my first and only manager…four hundred pound Teddy Reed you know. He saw fit to slip $50 out of a $150 pay check into his pocket. And I know that for a fact, because I dated the owner to the club and she happened to mention that it was a $150 pay check. And I said, oh yeah, so now I know where my manager took me. You learn as you go…

RR: And you never had a manager since.

CB: No, no. I couldn't get rid of him until he signed one of my checks…endorsed it rather and then I asked him for that or a release.

RR: I remember the first time I ever saw you on one of these Alan Freed shows in Toronto when you were coming through. And it was a big thing. You were by far the biggest star on the show. The show begins and you're the first act that goes on. I thought to myself even at that age…how come Berry wants to go on first?

CB: Well, it's not wants. Its where they put you.

RR: Let's cut ahead in time…a year later. I come and see an Alan Freed show. Then you had like two or three more hits after that. I go and see the show. You're still playing first. There had to be a message to this madness.

CB: OK. I was a good opening act. And it didn't matter to me.

RR: Because everybody was arguing, I've got to close the show. I've got to close the show.

CB: Because Chuck Berry didn't know that the star closes the show until maybe two years into his career. He began to look at the money the stars got and why they closed…they wanted to close. And still really…it doesn't matter today whether I close or open the show, because I'm going to try to rob everybody on the starship.

RR: Yeah. I thought there's got to be something to this. It's something I've got to understand. There must be some kind of special thing that he's on to that nobody else is getting or…

CB: If you go on first and you're not responsible for a riot if it happens and you're finished, and if the thing breaks up in the third act, you're still finished…remember it's a livelihood also.

RR: Did you stick around and watch the rest of the shows?

CB: Oh yeah, because you got to ride the bus to the next gig. And then not knowing that the better position and the better status of the artist is to play last. You know, last impression lasts. I didn't know these things, you know. In fact, when I went to the Paramount, my first New York gig, I didn't know that you changed. You know, you did five or six shows a night. I didn't know that you changed and the one suit that we had was satin and had the impression of seersucker. You know seersucker, and it was wrinkled, and I found out that they had irons and things to do your clothes up also and they would sew your clothes. All these little things, you know. And really, until I got to the Paramount, I didn't know that you had a room to yourself, like a dressing room. This is almost like home. All you have to have is a car and your guitar and you make it in the world. Just constantly playing every night…you have somewhere to sleep.

RR: How come you did so much work with Alan Freed. I mean you must have been on every one of those Alan Freed movies.

CB: Well now…

RR: Did you have a good relationship with the guy? I mean did you have a good business relationship with him?

CB: I'll tell you who had a good relationship with him. My record company gave the record to Alan Freed and it was either jumping from Cleveland to New York, whatever station it was, and, of course, then a little conversation, you played the record. I imagine that's what he got, because he played it and it was heard. Now the record might have had a little punch to it also, you know. And I imagine it did by living all these years. And that's where he is affiliated.

RR: He had that kind of power.

CB: Oh yeah, anybody did who had national exposure, and Leonard was tied in with him.

RR: Who's this. (Looking at photo.)

CB: That's my wife Themetta, and this is 1956 at home and they told me to pose at the piano. And this is the front of that house. And this is the famous pink Cadillac that used to get tickets by itself. This is a picture of…

RR: The young lovers.

CB: Yeah. This is in the courtship year. Six months we courted. And this is Ingrid, she's done an album with me. My daughter, and this is Melody, my second daughter. And here they are in school. And display of Sepia magazine, courtesy of Sepia. And this is *Rock, Rock, Rock*, the first movie I ever did. I was with Alan Freed. I don't know the figure on it. Something like $600. A lot of money then.

RR: "Roll Over Beethoven." How far did you go in school? I mean that's what made me think when I was a kid, I thought this guy must have gone to school or something. He's talking about Tchaikovsky and using these kind of lyrics.

CB: Okay. I went through high school. Got a bit of college, but not general education. I was all cosmetology. I went to college. Only for cosmetology...hair dressing.

RR: Really. This one right here. "Need strong Elvis Presley material for session coming up shortly. Would appreciate your contacting me as soon as possible. Regards, Freddie Beenstock, Elvis Presley music." They were asking you to write a song then for Elvis Presley.

CB: That's why I save that telegram.

RR: See the thing for me. Elvis Presley/Chuck Berry thing. The big thing for me is...why I was such a huge fan of yours. You could write the songs, you sang the songs, you played wicked guitar, it was just so much more all-around thing. Elvis never wrote a song you know. He could play a little guitar and everything, nice singer, but on a musician level, from my point of view, it was much more significant, the music you were doing. From what I can remember, I don't remember anybody else at that time being that all around, who wrote that kind of...that many songs, that many good songs, who could play as well as you and performed.

CB: I going to say the same thing right here because you...

RR: I know, I know, I don't mean to embarrass you by saying this, I just didn't...

CB: I tell you, I love lyrics, and I couldn't push a lyric without playing it, because I felt the move behind, the ingredients behind it, so I did want to play behind my singing.

RR: On so many of the songs you played, this position on the guitar which I studied very carefully as a child, just that the size of your hands and everything, but (make music sound) where did that come from, where was your first? You said that everything you ever did, you heard somebody else do it first. Where did you hear that first?

CB: It was Boogie Woogie Number One. And I would say it came from mimicking the figure on a piano. Ah one, five and six…in rhythmic progression, and you can do the same thing on the guitar much more easy I found. It's a constant background you can sing to it.

RR: Did you ever hear anybody (plays music) before you did it?

CB: The guitar players I listened to were Charlie Christian and T. Bone Walker, who did most of his figures in the treble strings, and Muddy, one string.

RR: Who were the guys? I mean for me it was you. For you, who was it when you were getting into music say, I want to do what this guy does. This …

CB: I went a whole different ball game. Because my first inspiration was Nat Cole in high school. And no girlfriend, you know, because I always had a gift of gab and I always did like comedy you know, and poetry. Comedy is too silly for me and poetry is too serious, so I was left out until I got into show business. They come to you, you know.

RR: Nat King Cole… he was the heavy for you.

CB: Yeah, yeah. But without a voice, I could not come near Nat Cole, but it didn't keep me from mimicking or liking his music. Then there was the piano, by nature, one of my loves, and I listened to Albert Edmonds, Pete Johnson, and that put me on guitar. I wanted to play guitar, and I can walk and sing and talk, so Louis Jordan's guitarist, Carl Hogen, was the inspiration for most of my solos, "Carol", "Johnny B. Goode" and "Roll Over Beethoven." He had something in the center of a solo and I opened my song with it. And "Roll Over Beethoven" after it hit later on "Johnny B. Goode" hit, later "Carol" hit with the same solo.

RR: Was there anybody, anything that you had heard before you did "Maybelline" that said 'wait a minute?'

CB: Sure, sure. As a matter of fact, I have stood on the stage in the Cosmopolitan and thinking of how I could produce something like Little Richards "Tutti Fruiti," which was really sizzling at the time. And you know the main thing about it? I couldn't understand what they were saying. When I went in to writing "Maybelline," I had a desire and intention to speak the words. Sound real clear. Nat Cole taught me that. Nat Cole had a diction that was just superb. And you can hear every word he says, but when you're singing like "Roll Over Beethoven," you got to be distinct in order to get your message out.

RR: Especially with the number of words you were using.

CB: So if you have two words with four syllables, you got to say them with a bark.

RR: Speaking of Little Richard, here's the little devil right there (looking at photo). This is the one here. That's rock and roll music. This thing about writing about…I mean I don't know how old you were at this…

CB: I was twenty-nine when "Maybelline" came out. So "School Days" was maybe…

RR: You were twenty-nine when "Maybelline" came out?

CB: Yeah, I had a house, and a car, and two children.

RR: But how, what made you think to write songs about up in the morning and out to school?

CB: Because when I went out on the road, I found that over half of the audience was teenagers…kids that were in school. So if they support what you're singing, you play what people want, you know. In nightclubs I had nothing to sing, "Down the way when the lights are gay," you know. I sing nothing about school days. They know nothing about "Roll Over Beethoven," boogie woogie, or dance. When they feel something they can dance, so that's why sometimes Leonard Chess would speed up the record. Like I was twenty-nine years old when I did these records, and I'm sure I sound like a father because I was a father, but he would speed the records.

RR: This is the first I've ever heard of this.

CB: Yeah, when the guys hear the record, it makes you sound like it's a higher voice.

RR: With these consecutive hits, how long did that go on?

CB: My greatest years were from '55 when I started with "Maybelline," which was a smash, through to I'd say four years… okay '55–'59. And then it began to taper off because then at that time the hippie era came, the miniskirt era was coming in.

RR: In the sixties.

CB: Oh yeah. Beautiful years, you were there as a teenager yourself and you know, nobody ah, the music went up on the wall in the, what do they call it, in the liquid showings, and smoking became popular and I don't mean Kools. And the sexual revolution was coming in and long hair.

RR: But what did this have to do with you no longer making records. You said it went from …

CB: Don't forget I'm thirty-five now and still the way that society is moving into this freedom…however, I'll tell you one thing though, I never smoked or did drugs.

RR: You never did any drugs in your life?

CB: No, no, no, I wouldn't, and I advise all others if they're on it, try…I don't think they can…but try anyway. I just think too many of my friends, Joplin, Hendrix, you name it, some of the greats on the train, and I'm feeling fine without it.

RR: So what happened? All these hits are going bang, bang, bang, bang, bang and then you sound like the sexual revolution is going into focus. What happened? Did you run out of ideas? Did you stop recording? What did you do?

CB: I tell you what I did. I was continually being called to do dates. And so, as you see on these little charts, the fee for the dates constantly rose, for instance when I had my problems with the, ah, Indian girl, I was away for almost a couple of years. I went away making $1,200 a night. When I came back, the Beatles had come to America and my salary then was $2,000 a night from being away. Now if this is America, you stay away somewhere, you come back, you got more pay. I came back with "Nadine;" I came with there "No Particular Place To Go."

RR: Was the world…was it different then?

CB: Oh yes.

RR: I mean besides The Beatles and music evolving, you had been this huge star playing everywhere in the world, hits popping, inspiration. All of a sudden, bingo, you run into a brick wall, your life changes…

CB: No, no, no. Now let me tell you. Life didn't change. If you call it a brick wall when I went away?

RR: Yeah.

CB: Okay when I went away, number one, finished high school. Number two, took five business courses…well I took accounting, business management. When I came back I found out what I had, which was a corporation. I knew what accounting was. I'm better qualified….

RR: That's what I wanted to ask you. I didn't want to bring it up if you didn't want to talk about it, but I wanted to ask you how you utilized that education.

CB: This is the way. It's easy to count my blessings as well as to count my misfortunes. And I came out quite better. Don't forget I had a little bank account that I had to maintain.

RR: Did you write any music?

CB: I'm telling you. I came out with "Nadine" and "No Particular Place to Go," but finally in '70, which was six years later, here's "My Ding-A-Ling"…smash hit!! Recorded in England you know. Okay, they say, he made a comeback. Well frankly other than my absence, I never left. I'm heavy into real estate, because that's the only place I see to spend money is to invest money that is lucratively…and exploiting my wealth. I don't have someone to take care of it and that takes quite a bit of your time. So, I have the investment company that I run, real estate, and then I have Chuck Berry Music, that runs my music. But back to "My Ding A Ling," at this time "My Ding A Ling" was a hit. I bought more property and I'm into about three different people now, a business man, a musician and you say a writer…they say father of rock and roll, and quite busy. Now, someone's trying to make me a movie star. I don't know. I might make it.

CHAPTER TWO
Chuck Berry, Bo Diddley, & Little Richard

TAYLOR HACKFORD: This next section of bonus material from the DVD is probably my favorite. The witnesses to history. Except these witnesses are actual creators: the creators of rock and roll, the people who defined a new American art form. Because Chuck is generally considered to be the father of rock and roll, I got a lot of people, his contemporaries, to agree to talk about him in this film. And while I had them, I decided to ask them about their own music, about the definition of their own sound and what they were feeling at the birth of this art form, because in '55 and '56, that was the birth of rock and roll, and we're fifty years later right now, so I believe this to be truly historic. You see, Little Richard, Bo Diddley, and Chuck Berry around a piano talking about what it was like to be black and completely create an art form that took white America by storm. You know it wasn't easy for these guys, but they were the creators, and to see these men, never before together, never talking like this, for an hour discussing this, I think is historic.

CHUCK BERRY: You know I actually heard "Tutti Frutti" before I ever went to Chess to do "Maybelline," and I loved it. And you were one of the hit founders, and although Alan Freed coined it and many of the brothers and some of the white boys helped bring it about, and the continuity of it, believe me, there are few of us left.

LITTLE RICHARD: I'm so proud to see black people get together, like this is the first chance I've had to do this in my whole life of all the years I've been in the business. You know, I've been with all the white artists and the different people that didn't start what is happening today and yesterday either. And to see you and Bo Diddley here and to, you know, I had something to do and I told my manager I have to cancel this, because I felt bad that I talked with everybody else and here's my two brothers and you're putting them up and I had to do this, even if the other thing had to be cancelled.

CB: You are here.

LR: I'm glad to get this opportunity to speak with you and Bo Diddley. I mean this is something that the world has never seen. I mean the world has had this chance to see you, and I and Bo together, you know, it just…I was just telling Bo, I'm just so sorry and saddened as I travel the world. Bo Diddley, like through Europe…he's so huge, ah, through those countries and when he gets back here, I told him, you don't hear nothing. This man is, he's never gotten any recognition at all and he's an innovator. He's an emancipator, you know, he's a great, great person and a fantastic musician and a great writer. In fact, I never heard no one write songs like you and Bo Diddley in my life. You feel what you write. It's so fantastic.

BO DIDDLEY: You see a lot of people don't understand. People come up to me and ask me…they probably ask Chuck the same thing. "Are you Bo Diddley? How did you get started? Or how did Chuck Berry get his beat," I said "we'll go find Chuck. He can explain it to you." He was busy working on trying to get his thing together, while I was trying to figure out how I could get in there and get on the bandwagon also. And somehow or other we both emerged somewhere around the same time.

CB: You know, I got a slogan for it whenever anybody says "how did you get started?" I always say, "very slowly. Very slowly."

LR: I like that.

BD: That's the truth. It was hard. Like you were saying a little while ago, a lot of people think what we are doing is easy. There's nothing easy about it to sit down and try and create a product that you can put out a record as a record. You got to set your mind and listen to people's conversation and take a little word from here. You can hear a conversation where some guy can speak one word and you can run home and you can write a tune from that one little word that he spoke…the way that he used it. But then there are a lot of people. I wasn't as fortunate as Chuck Berry to write the type of songs, but I wrote different type of lyrics.

When he came up with "Maybelline" and I heard this reggae guitar, it started me to listening. Listening to his whole scene that was coming to emerge…it would come up and it became a thing.

CB: Bo Diddley was a hit before I ever went to Chess. Now quit complimenting me.

BD: We was in there together.

CB: Speaking of Georgia. That's where you're from.

LR: I'm from Macon, Georgia.

LR: I first started recording for RCA Victor and they didn't have no rock and roll, white or black. I was on RCA Victor before Elvis Presley, but it was called Camden. If you was black you was put on Camden. And if you was white you were on RCA. So I was on a label called Camden.

BD: But that's what Chess had going. See, Aristocrat was for the black artists and Chess and Checker was for anybody else. Willie Dixon broke it up. Because he understood what was going on. I was just a young dude off the street corners of Chicago. I didn't know nothing. You know, they said play and I said how loud.

LR: That's what I did. When they put me on Camden, I thought I was going to be on RCA. You know, I didn't know no difference. I was a little guy from Georgia...real young, really too young. I didn't even sign the contract. My mother signed it. I had my mother sign the contract. We was poor. My mother had twelve children. I used to play at a white club called Annie's Tick Tock...all white. Yeah baby, I was the only brown, I'll never forget it...I was always smiling.

CB: It took them twenty years to find out brown was beautiful.

LR: Yeah, that's right. No, they was going to the beach every summer. You know nobody's pleased with what God gave them. The white man go to the beach to get this every summer and we going to the cosmetic shop to get something to get... you know.

TH: This music came out in '54 or '55. Where did it come from?

LR: Well this was '54/'55 because it just got to be known, but I was singing rock and roll way before that. I was singing rock and roll when I was a boy and, in fact, nobody wanted to hear me. I was singing in a club with a lady called Gladys Wiggins in a band. I was singing one song...they put me out of the club because everybody was singing blues and what I was singing was really...they didn't like it. But I went to white clubs and they liked it, but the black kids wanted the blues because B. B. King was singing blues. He was singing low-down blues and Muddy Waters was singing Elmore James on a low-down blues album.

BD: They had not even coined it rock and roll.

LR: No…they didn't put a title on it.

BD: In fact that didn't come up until Alan Freed did. Alan Freed tagged it…the music that we all came up with and everybody was listening to, rock and roll…the minute that the white kids started picking up guitars, we couldn't get records played on the radio, and I remember hearing Phil Chess, this guy said "you know what, if we could get a white kid to play this song, we could get it played," because the radio stations were all caucasians. They wouldn't play black music, so they said okay, so all of a sudden you got Carl Perkins popped up, Elvis Presley, Gene Vincent…they all come out of with their own records…they were playing rockabilly. All of a sudden we became a no/no. What is this? This is devil music.

CB: You know, really the way I heard it from Alan Freed when he was tipsy, you know, he drank a lot. He ran a dance in Cleveland. And the way we danced, danced together you know, cheek to cheek, and not always the same cheek, you know. We were rocking with each other; we were dancing closely and rolling around. Sometimes the barrel-house roll and, of course, Freed that's where he got that term…we were rocking and rolling.

LR: Me personally, I had never heard about Elvis Presley, Gene Vincent, and I'm from the South, down there, and I'm from Georgia and not far from Tennessee, and I used to sing at a little black club called the New Euro Club. I never heard anything about them. They sang country music. When I saw them, they were singing country music…Bill Monroe and the Blue Grass Boys. They were singing country music because even after the years with Camden Records, then left Camden and went with Peacock Records…they didn't know what to do with what I was singing. Then finally when I went with Specialty and made "Tutti Frutti," black records wouldn't get played on white stations even at the period.

CB: Yeah, but you know what the kids found him. You would be surprised how word of mouth goes around, and I think that's just about when transistors came into being.

LR: Yeah, that its. That's when I was covered by Pat Boone. That's when Fats Domino was covered by everybody but the kitchen sink. That's when Laverne Baker was covered by everybody but the maid.

BD: That was a bad time…there was a bad overhanging there when the thing became separated. R&B became what we was doing, and rock and roll was what the white kids was doing.

CB: Yeah, you mean we moved and separated. We weren't called popular music. We weren't put in that…we were called rhythm and blues

LR: R&B stands for Real Black. R&B means that a black guy had real great music. If he was white, they had…he was POP: Pop. If you was black it was R&B, which means it was black. It was real black and if you was white, it was POP.

BD: I just learned that.

LR: Yeah, oh I've been knowing it for years. And I know when I used to go to places and sing, the white girls were screaming. They did not want no black image over those white kids, especially the white girls. They didn't care about white boys. The only two people that have been in captivity has been the black nannies and white ladies. What's happened is when I started with "Whop, baba loo bob" and Pat Boone covered it,

I was "WHOO" all over the place, and so I remember Arthur Goldsburg, he says they put my record on the top station and then here come Pat Boone. The white kids wanted mine because it was real rough and raw and Pat Boone has this smooth (imitate) and I had (sings), you know, I had gut to mine, and so the white kids would take mine and put it in the drawer and put his on top of the dresser. I was in the same house, but in a different location. That's really what happened at that period of time.

CB: That's true. In fact, that's how a lot of white artists came into being in rock and roll from playing, ah, rhythm and blues music.

BD: You had enough people doing new things and stuff like this helped to keep it going from generation to generation, because somewhere along the road, we gonna got shoved aside.

CB: Those were pay days.

BD: Right and we got shoved...wait a minute we'll be back. We're gonna go and get this.

LR: But, you know, that was good to some extent, but I was mad. When Pat Boone came out, man I was mad. I was going to go to Nashville and find him. I wasn't kidding at the time, because he was stomping my progress. I wanted to be famous and here this man done came and took my song. And not only did he take "Tutti Frutti," but he even take "Long Tall Sally." I got to do something about it, and in later years I thought about that and said that was good, but not back then. I thought ooh I can't stand him. And I got older, I got bolder. Yeah! And I started rubbing his shoulders.

BD: Amen.

LR: That's not the way it goes. And don't you accept that no more.

BD: I don't know if Chuck felt that way. I felt about the same way you did. I learned that, hey, I am important, very important, because if these cats think a lot of me to imitate me, that's pretty good. There are some guys that can't even get arrested.

LR: They said "where did you come from and where you going?"

CB: You have been laughing since 1955.

LR: Oh I was laughing…since 1945. I have to laugh. Remember I'm from Georgia, and you have to laugh or you have to cry. So I wanted to laugh.

CB: You know Little Richard there are some things we couldn't laugh about back there. You know.

LR: There was a lot of things I couldn't laugh at because my dad got killed back then during that period. And I had a lot of friends that died back then during that period. A lot of racism back then during my career. Everybody wasn't like that though. But there is a lot of people that was and that made it hard for the people who wasn't. They made it uncomfortable for the people who had to suffer for that.

CB: In Georgia?

LR: Yes, in my hometown of Macon.

CB: I have news for you. It was also in my hometown in St. Louis.

BD: That's no big deal…it was in Chicago. In New York and Los Angeles and Chicago. It was worse in Mississippi.

CB: And I think it was raining all over the world. You have any bad embarrassments.

LR: Yeah, police take me off the stage in Augusta, Georgia, a few miles from my hometown, and beat me with blackjacks, but I had so much hair it just bounced off me. The police said "you making music to these white kids." That's what they said. "You singing nigger music to white kids." And that's what they'd say to Elvis. When Elvis went to different cities, they'd say "that's nigger music." So when you go to town, they said, "stop this boy from coming in this area with all this nigger music." He don't need to say that over there. I have them stop me and block me and then pop me. You understand me. They took me to jail…I got bail.

BD: I seen situations like that. I been in the midst of situations where we played in Georgia, and I don't know why at that particular time, Georgia had this real record of being bad news. I remember the time that I was going down the highway and it was like bad news to have a pretty car. And I should have know better. And, you know, its with Irish potatoes on your head. So, you know, I was made to get out of the car… me and my band and because we didn't have no liquor, they pulled out their guns and said since you all musicians, you entertain us and we'll let you go. So we jumped out, and one cat said, "what's the rags for." Because everybody used to fix their hair really nice. We call it processes. We couldn't get up in the morning and expect for it to look the same way.

LR: Doorags…I remember that.

BD: You had dudes coming down the street with rags on their hair just like they do today with all these little nets on their heads, look funny.

CB: They made you entertain.

BD: Oh yeah…and dance.

CB: They made you dance?

BD: Oh yeah. With a 98 in your face. And a shotgun.

LR: What did you do?

BD: You did flips. In order to deliver the music, we went to some terrible ordeals.

TH: When it first started. When you first came out with "Tutti Frutti," did you think the music was going to last?

LR: No, I didn't because rhythm and blues to me…rock and roll is really rhythm and blues up tempo. When I hear people like Muddy Waters talked about so much. Elmo James and Lew Walters in Atlanta, Georgia…we be there together in Atlanta, and, you know, when I went to see all these people, Chuck Berry, Bo Diddley, and Jackie Princeton. When you go back with all this stuff, way back, you know rock and roll, rhythm and blue up tempo.

BD: Boogie Woogie.

LR: Boogie Woogie…its all Boogie Woogie, and people are doing it to this day.

BD: Let me tell you something. Let me say something, Chuck Berry, I sit back and I listen. I said, "this cat's got some kind of something that is going on that I cannot do. So, I'm not going to jump on his thing and mess with it, and I'm going to try and create my own."

CB: You can't duck walk.

BD: You might not realize it, but Chuck is a magic to what you're doing. You could take two saxophone players and one of them could handle his sax and make more things out of it than the other one can. And the other might have had more training. What I mean by that is that evidently you experimented to try to create something that didn't sound like somebody else's.

CB: True.

BD: He's original.

LR: You are too Bo.

BD: Yeah, well I created my own little thing. I can't play nothing this man do.

LR: Yeah, he do his own thing. The first song of his I try to sing is "Maybelline."

CB: I been playing it for thirty-two years and I never heard anybody do your songs like you…never.

You were the original and nobody can do it.

LR: And nobody's guitar sounds like Bo's either. I tell you something, Chuck Berry's songs are really, God knows… I've never heard no rock and roll singer…black or white, red, brown, or yellow…Chuck Berry is a poet. He's a living poet in his own lifetime. And I thank God that he's alive today…a great person, a great father, a great son and a great artist. He's contributed so much to the music field. And Chuck is not a person to seek publicity. He don't seek glory. He don't seek to be heard or known and this you can see. Wherever the microphone is, I will speak.

CB: Oh yes, brother, go on.

LR: But Chuck's done more than anybody. He takes care of himself and he's a very private person. He's self-sufficient in every way. Spiritually, physically, and financially, and mentally.

Chuck Berry is a poet. He is a poet. He's a songwriter. He writes poems. He's a lover.

CB: I'm getting out of here.

LR: He writes to rhythms that make you dance. He tells the truth. His songs are not gimmicks, but they're the truth, in force and in energy. With a whole lot of life to them. You know my favorite song with Chuck is all of them (laughs). Not to put Bo down. To the God of Abraham, Isaac, and Jacob, my God and I love so much of that…I keep the Sabbath every Saturday from sundown to…he's my favorite rock artist and he always has been, and I think that I never told the world this, but his rhythm is all I can sing myself too. But Chuck Berry is really fantastic, and I think that…but I give it to Bo. When I first heard Bo Diddley sing, I was in the middle of a Pentecostal Church. And I said "he shout just like my mother do." And to see all of these people get together. You see rock and roll, to be truthful, it is the title that Chuck Berry say…Alan Freed is a wonderful guy. I used to work for him in New York at the Paramount. Alan is a good guy. I really loved Alan Freed. He was a guy who showed no racism to me. I never seen nothing like that. He was a young Jewish guy that was a brother and a lover…I loved Alan. He was one of the greatest I ever met. And…I just loved the way that he did what he did and he did a good job, a great job. If you're Chinese, I'd love to eat rice with you.

TH: At the beginning of rock and roll you guys were trying to get your music out and trying to get it heard and having to deal with the business world.

BD: Me, myself, I didn't know anything about it, the business end of it. That didn't faze me at all. All I wanted was a record.

There was a record company a couple of blocks away from my house which was affiliated with Chess, I started trying to figure out how much I was going to get later.

CB: The main thing in the beginning is you just want to hear yourself.

BD: I just wanted to hear myself on the radio. I think I burned up two or three radios, you know, trying to find the record that was being played, which was "Hey, Bo Diddley" and "I'm a Man." And, ah, money, you know. I sat up all night looking at the contracts, you know, trying to figure out how we're going to make any money out of two.

CB: Half a cent...

BD: Half a cent...you had to sell three records to make a penny or something. I was getting on the air. How could you divide up half a cent on a record. Somebody was getting ahead, but I couldn't figure out.

LR: You had to sell two records to make a penny.

BD: Right. And I started looking around, and I told my mother and she says, "you ain't going to make any money with that." I said, "oh, they said I'd make a lot of money." She said "yeah."

CB: She see that you didn't. The record costs fifty-nine cents then. But there were fifty-eight other pennies going somewhere.

LR: I couldn't understand the contract. I didn't read that far.

BD: Today you got a lot of artists. Some of them are almost in the same shape we are, because they got so many lawyers and advisors and they got managers and they got assistant managers and they got another manager...all this kind of stuff. When they get through, they owe somebody. So some of them ain't better off than we were. But then there are some that are getting paid. Well, that's the bottom line, getting paid.

LR: I have a manager now, and I wish I had one then.

BD: I had one but he didn't know...he was more producer than manager. A lot of managers didn't take you back then.

LR: All I wanted to do was be famous. I just wanted to get famous. I just wanted to make it and go back to my hometown....

CB: You sure did it, you sure did it, because this is Little Richards.

LR: I'm a star without a car.

BD: That became a monument within itself. That little holler. There are a whole bunch of dudes out here who choke trying to do...

LR: I used to teach it...when the Beatles came from Hamburg, Germany, from Liverpool, I used to teach it to them.

BD: Speaking of England, I remember when I first went to London. Me and you were on the show together with Dwayne Eddie. And, ah...

LR: Everly Brothers...ah, Mick Jagger.

BD: What I was getting ready to say...

CB: Louie Jordan, Joe Turner, Caldonia with the shake, rattle and roll...this was the beginning of the music venturing over into the white area.

BD: Fats Domino too, man. Ah, Laverne Baker, what she was doing back then. Ah, Ruth Brown.

TH: Richard, when rock and roll came out...the three of you came out. There was something very distinctive. What was the difference. What was the unique element of rock and roll?

LR: You mean when we were traveling? Just the sound you mean? Well, first of all rock and roll to me the music was faster...it was much faster, and at that time, being real young, it was energy. I remember the young kids from my hometown...they was tired of hearing "Pennies from Heaven." I just be looking for pennies, you know, trying to find them. I believe in heaven...that's what I believe. But at that time, the type of songs was Billie Eckstein.

LR: And the kids wanted more energy. You know, you sitting down and used to have little things, and I used to play the piano and invite them over to my house. My dad gave me this upright piano and it was the raggiest piano you ever seen. And I started playing it, and they would dance and sing with it, so then I got this contract in Atlanta Georgia...I worked at the theater sometimes. It was a vaudeville. I don't know if you ever heard of Silas Green, from New Orleans and the Florida Blossom show. I was with a show called Sugar Foot Sam from Ala-bam.

CB: You talk about a poet. You were one, and you know it.

LR: I got on, and so they had me dressed all kind of ways and the music was so dead like at that time to me all I got to do is back the hearse up and bring the coffin. And so rock and roll to me was like an explosion. It was a great big explosion and to see it still lasting today, which I never thought what is happening would happen and its back full force again. In fact, it never left. I just went through other people's hands.

CB: How good did it feel when you went to the department store in downtown Macon, and you walked in there and you heard, "Tutti Frutti"?

LR: It felt so good. I felt so good just hearing "Tutti Frutti" period. Because my mama had all these kids and the first time

I heard "Tutti Frutti," I heard it on the radio 'cause I had went to New Orleans, and I came back, and I was at a club called the Club Tijuana in New Orleans. Did you ever hear of that? I was there, and so it had a club called the Pelican Club and I came back, and so the kids in my hometown didn't know that my name was Little Richard. They were still calling me Bro, you know. And so when I heard the new record, I said that's me. Because it's strange, the first record I made didn't even get on the radio in my home town. Couldn't even get air play in my hometown. I don't know why. I just went up and said, "shit, you got to play my record." And they did not play my record.

CB: Sky McFadden told me once he could sit on a corner and eat watermelon all day and he wouldn't draw flies in his hometown.

CB: Bo you was talking about a while ago how the rock and roll came about.

BD: Well it had to be Alan Freed and a couple of more DJ's that I can't…

CB: Allowed it to be played over the white airwaves. That's when it really started.

BD: See because…well, Alan Freed. I remember Alan Freed telling me about somebody throwing bricks through his window. He's gonna get run out of the neighborhood because he defied the system. Well, I call it the system because the system is the one that allowed them to do it in the first place. You understand. He defied them. All of a sudden our good friend, Dick Clark, came up with the television thing and started putting us on American Bandstand.

CB: Not on the stage through, we could never…

BD: No, you couldn't dance. Because the station was owned by people I think that prohibited him.

CB: Why was it done. Answer that for the record. Why was it done...he didn't want it to be done. He was the master of ceremonies. Anybody that allows it to stand and maintain...

LR: Well, I think this. It was a still a little Jewish boy that got it over the country, named Alan Freed.

CB: Amen.

LR: He still got it over the country and he did a good job. I love you, Alan.

BD: It wasn't anything that we was doing was so strong, it was just that people were so slow.

LR: You was black. You was black.

CB: Tell him again. Will you tell him again.

LR: You was black and they didn't wants that black image over their kids. You was a hero. And the kids was looking up to you, and they didn't want their kids looking up to that big old breezy black guy out of Georgia, out of Mississippi, out of Chicago. They wanted their kids to look smooth white boy, looking pretty and all dooty and looking rooty. You know.

BD: I wouldn't put it exactly like that.

LR: That's the way it was.

BD: But Beethoven went out the window.

CB: No...he only stepped aside. He gave me room. A few of the rock and roll...see the music was so free. A few of the rock and rollers, music being free, they wanted to do their thing. And their thing might have been a little sexy or a little, ah, dusty or whatever. When those were the records that they used as a crutch to kill all of the music. What's wrong with "School Days"? You know, but if you say Baby, ah, this and that, then it's a little shady you know. But don't say all of its rock and roll and throw all of it out.

LR: It's a message music. It's message music in rhythm. You know, ah, its just like, it was bad because it was black at the time. I mean the truth is the truth. If a white boy sang the same song, he'd have been on TV shows. When I did a bop, I didn't bop with my head, I bopped with my bottom.

BD: Well, what did they do with me and Elvis Presley.

LR: They didn't show him either.

BD: Yes they did. When I did Bo Diddley on Ed Sullivan and then he came on. They cut me off.

LR: They cut your bottom and showed your head.

CB: Let me tell you something. They paid me $20,000 to go to Memphis and do a tribute to Elvis. I took a white country singer with me. You know here's Elvis, Tennessee. Guess what, we were singing like "Memphis, Tennessee." She was singing the higher part. I was singing the lower part. They are to stand up here, Mr. Berry. And they wanted her to stand ... we're singing here together. They didn't show any of it, because they had them to show us together.

BD: Most black kids did not know what was going on. They were in a shade themselves…a lot of them. They didn't know nothing. When we started jumping up and people like Jimmy Clanton, he came along, and he finds "what is this black-and-white music you all talking about?" And I said, "you haven't heard. You don't know what's happening." He says, "no man. All I want to do is sing." We were all eased into this separation type thing. And then when we found it out, everybody was running.

LR: It was all circumstance. Victims of circumstance. Because I've been colored blind all my life.

BD: Amen.

LR: I've always had white friends. I played with white kids when I was a little boy. Had good white friends. You should see some of my family. Oh, Chuck it was terrible. We used to tour all over the country in buses. I remember when I did a tour with Fats Domino, Tina Turner...

CB: How many on the show?

LR: About thirty. All black. And I think there was two whites. And we'd go to the cities, and we really would have a time finding a place to stay. Just finding somewhere to stay because we were black. We'd go to homes and houses of people. Get out and back inside the bus.

CB: You been on some of those shows where it was thirty white and thirty black.

BD: I remember the time, you know, we did some bus tours together you and I. And I think you and Richard and I...too much power.

CB: Too much power.

BD: Anyway, I remember the time we went to Augusta, Georgia, and the bus driver was named John Pelligrini. He's a white fellow out of Jersey. He dropped us off in the black neighborhood, so we could get something to eat, and we waited on the bus. So some cab driver comes and says, "y'all bus driver's in jail." We said "what. Bus Driver's in jail. For what?" Well, he kept riding around the block in this neighborhood around here, with them New York license plates on there and they got him over there. So me, the smart aleck, you know, I'm going to go get him out of jail. And I take Charlie Carpenter with me. Remember Charlie Carpenter? We go down there. Anyway, we go down there to get this white man out of jail, you know what I'm saying.

CB: A white bus driver?

BD: Yes. No way José. Boy that was the word that came out of the sergeant's mouth. Boy, you take your money and get out of here. No nigger's gonna come down here and get no white man out of jail. And I said, "wow, here I am pleading for these people and they jumpin' up and down, and this kid's probably going to be at the show and probably the first one to buy a ticket. And you mean to tell me this is what we dealing with?"

CB: He may have been the promoter. We sure did have a problem with black and white years ago. And they'd send these flyers out before you, and you'd go into a place and black and white, they can't deal with it. They don't care who it is. And they turned you away because they found out.

LR: At some of the shows I did in the early days when I was drawing more blacks, they would have white spectators and they used to play like that too. And the white people would jump over the balcony and come.

LR: But I had to go to court like you did Bo, and the Judge asked me "what did I have to say for myself." What do I have to say for myself. Everything. And he said "order in the court." I said, "that's what you need in here. I haven't seen any of that since I've been here." And so he told me if I did that one more time, they were going to put me out...they were going to lock me up. He told me I was crazy. I'll never forget that.

BD: He told you your hair was too pretty.

LR: He told me my hair was too long. He says "are you a man. What are you?"

CB: I was crazy. I did a song "Crazy…"

LR: That was Elvis. He was a very good friend of mine. Elvis was a really terrific person. He was a lovable guy. He was real nice. One time I saw him…he was a little shy, but when he saw me, he took off his shades. He told me I had pretty skin. I'll never forget that. He came back to my dressing room. I was appearing at a hotel in Vegas, and Elvis to me, he was a fantastic performer. He was an electrifying entertainer. He was a great entertainer, and a great human being. I really loved him.

CB: He was good-looking too.

LR: He was beautiful…he was very beautiful. He was handsome. He was a nice guy…one of the nicest people I've ever met…black or white.

CB: You know I never saw him take off on the guitar.

LR: Elvis to me was a great entertainer. He was not a country pianist, but I'm not either. And he's not a country guitarist. He more trying to get a show across, but Elvis to me was not what you'd call a great guitar player, but he was a great person and he was a great entertainer. He knew how to play to accompany himself.

BD: He really learned how to entertain after he came out of the service.

LR: Yes, well that's when I met him.

BD: He became interesting to me when he came out of the service.

LR: Well that's when I met him. And Gene Dixon was very good.

CB: I knew Gene.

LR: He started a lot of fights though. He put me out of his car on the highway. I never forget it. He put me out of his car and I wouldn't get out. I wouldn't get out on the highway.

CB: Who is the most beautiful woman you have ever laid your eyes on? Take your time.

LR: Besides my mother...

CB: Okay, who is the most beautiful man?

LR: ME!!! I couldn't let that one get by, 'cause you now that's the truth folks.

CB: *Hail! Hail! Rock 'N' Roll.*

LR: *Hail! Hail! Rock 'N' Roll.* Aint that the truth, Bo. I am gorgeous. Look. It don't mean a thing. Thank you, Chuck. This has been so nice. You know. This is something...this will be when we're gone on, this will still be in the world, you know. And I just want to say that you've been inspirational all my life. Ever since I met you. You're so for real, Bo. You've been for real always.

BD: See I want to tell you something. When you were doing all of the stuff before you made the change over, you know, I used to stand back in the back. And I don't watch nobody, you know. And I watch him all the time, you know. And I watch you. But there are very few people that I'll stand and watch their show, because they're fascinating, you know. Now you can catch a guy that's out there doing a whole thing of work and playing all behind his back and fighting the guitar. To me he's hungry. It's a wasted effort. Make your instrument play something. That's what you do and that's what Chuck Berry does. He make his guitar say something. That's the reason why he's Chuck Berry.

LR: I be seeing what you mean when I be touring with you. I used to feel you. I used to love that.

BD: Let me see what you're going to do next.

LR: And let me tell you something. I used to watch you too.

CB: You know what he saying. You've changed. You've changed into rock. You changed rock. You went back home.

LR: Most black singers that's where their roots are...in the church. I call my music now a message song. Chuck, it's just beautiful to have the opportunity to sit down with you and Bo...two legends, the rock and roll legends that you don't hear enough about. I wish Fats Domino was here. I really do. A living legend, and I'm just glad to be one of them with you all. And I just pray to God that we'll all be here a long time, and this isn't our last go 'round, you know.

CB: May we live a hundred years.

A few thoughts about Chuck from two other legends:

JOHNNIE JOHNSON: (in separate short interview): These guys are the architects of rock and roll. Now coming up in an era where, ah, you weren't allowed to do things or you weren't expected to do things, ah, leaves you with the feeling that when you do get an opportunity to do something, you've got to do it better than anybody could possibly do it. That's how most black performers actually lived. They know they just can't do the job well, they have to do it better than anybody else, or else they're not going to get a shot. It's a very bizarre thing. Rock and roll is still considered a white genre in music, where the guys that actually invented the art form are black. If you're a black person playing rock and roll, it's almost like some kind of novelty or something. Even to this day, you know, he's black, he's rocking. Yeah.

He wasn't much different to me. But I could see how Chuck acted with other people, and I knew he had a chip on his shoulder. He was angry as to how the law had treated him and thought everyone wanted to cheat him. He was definitely a different person after he came out of prison.

CARL PERKINS: Never saw a man (Chuck) so changed. He had been an easygoing man before, the kinda guy you could sit in the dressing room and swap licks and jokes. In England he was cold and bitter. It wasn't just jail, it was years of one nighters, grinding it out like that can kill a man, but I figure it was mostly the jail.

CHAPTER THREE
Making the Deal with Chuck Berry

WHEN BEGINNING A DEAL *with an artist, one usually is told to talk to a lawyer or an agent, but in the case with Chuck Berry, he would negotiate everything himself and had done so for years. And, as we didn't realize at the time, if there was a way of interpreting the contract to squeeze more money out of the deal, he would do it and he did.*

The Chuck Berry film, Hail! Hail! Rock 'N' Roll, *was to be a follow-up to the Cinemax television series of intimate musical performances that my company, Delilah Films, produced. The first one was* Carl Perkins & Friends—Blue Suede Shoes: A Rockabilly Session, *featuring the likes of Eric Clapton, George Harrison, Ringo Starr, Dave Edmunds and Rosanne Cash. Cinemax had agreed to buy the TV rights for a Chuck Berry special, and so we approached Suzie Petersen who had recently started a new division at Universal Pictures to sell the home video rights. I had previously sold her other films,* The Doors: Live in Europe 1968 *and* Women in Rock. *My first documentary,* The Compleat Beatles, *had been released theatrically. My lawyer, Albert Spevak, and I worked directly with Chuck for a TV and video deal which probably took six months, at which point my line producer Tom Adelman and I decided that Chuck Berry being a legend really deserved a theatrical feature film. This decision would lead to more endless negotiations that continued through development, production, and postproduction of the film. The challenge of casting the film took a toll on the sanity of all those involved, and propositions of sex in exchange for paying our star more money was commonplace in dealing with Mr. Berry. It was the first deal at a new wing of Universal, so there was a lot riding on it for Suzie Petersen and her team as well as my company.*

SUZIE PETERSEN: I remember how horrendous it was at times…I thought my job was at stake. We were doing projects for both pay television and home video and not theatrical, but we were a very fledgling group at Universal then, trying to develop programming in those two areas. And then Stephanie Bennett and I had talked and developed some music ideas, and so I think we proceeded on that basis as I recall. I mean way before Taylor Hackford was attached to the film or even Keith Richards. I think we were talking to Robbie Robertson then. We weren't a producing entity yet, so really it was, an acquisition, but because the show hadn't been produced yet, we also had to be involved in the actual production and to be honest, we were not fully equipped to do so. So it was an interesting learning process.

ALBERT SPEVAK: The agreement that was signed between Delilah Films and Chuck Berry on November 21, 1985, was the result of rather extensive back and forth negotiations, but the interesting thing about it was that it was a full production agreement. And essentially Delilah Films was doing the film for Chuck Berry. Under this agreement, Chuck actually owned the copyright in the film. He was guaranteed over a period of time $300,000.00. It was a very tight production window and it was done in 1985. The meetings and the concepts and all of the discussions we were going to have, had to happen by early January 1986, and the concert would be done by June 1986, which isn't too far off from when it was actually filmed.

At the time it was really going to be a television pay-TV and home video release, and Delilah's fee was relatively modest at $40,000.00 a year. Delilah had a participation for a number of years in the profits of the film. And then, after I think about six years, everything went back to Chuck Berry. So this was frankly the way to get into business with Chuck Berry, and it was as much probably as anything an announcement. It was "okay, let's do this film and make a few bucks and move on." Who were going to be the guests and who was going to be a musical director. Chuck had approval over that...Chuck had approval over all the guests and it was a pretty modest deal, with Chuck making a bunch of money for showing up and doing a TV Show. That's pretty much what it was. So that was the concept of the original agreement from 1985.

We discovered that with the Carl Perkins film, and later with the Roy Orbison film, having a musical director added credibility that attracted stars and helped bring the music together. The obvious person we initially thought of was Robbie Robertson, a mutual friend Scott Richardson and also a musician, and set up a meeting.

STEPHANIE BENNETT: Tom and I and Scott went to Robbie's studio/office and asked Robbie if he would be interested in being the musical director for the film. Robbie wasn't sure if he was the right person, but simultaneously I think he suggested that a more appropriate person, might be Keith Richards.

As luck would have it, Keith was available because Mick Jagger had decided to do a solo album and The Rolling Stones were on another hiatus. Tom Adelman and I started thinking if we could get a major director on board, we could sell it as a feature. I went back to Suzie Petersen at MCA/Universal, and said, "what if we get a big name director, would this be something that would be interesting to you?" Suzie's eyes lit up. And so, Tom and I went in search of the right director. We met about five directors and ultimately Taylor Hackford was the one that Chuck choose to be the director. He had done *The Idolmaker*, which explored the drama of the music scene at the time.

SP: With Taylor it was a fantastic idea because he had early in his career been very involved in music documentary kinds of things, and so bringing him in kicked it up a notch and brought a lot more interest from our theatrical group.

SB: Our carefully negotiated deal for a television special with Chuck was now changing to a theatrical film. And so, of course we had to go back to Chuck and enter into a new renegotiation.

AS: All of a sudden our simple TV agreement was turned into chaos. So that's really what opened up a can of worms. We had to go to Chuck and say, "okay the good news is that we're going to do it as a feature film. The bad news is we've got to change the whole structure of the agreement," and that's what started a series of the first round of renegotiations, because also we changed the schedule, and we had had some very specific dates in there that we had to meet. We had to get into the details in the renegotiation.

DICK ALLEN: Well, the contract was not exactly as he felt it was negotiated and if people are giving him an option or a way that he can ask for more money, he will do so.

TOM ADELMAN: The contract was a moving target and Chuck had it and Stephanie in his cross hairs on a daily basis

SB: This would be a daily occurrence. One day the crew arrived at Berry Park where we were filming the rehearsals and the gates were locked, and inside was probably two million dollars worth of movie equipment.

TAYLOR HACKFORD: On day two the same thing happened, another renegotiation. So again, we are just waiting for our star. I've talked to Stephanie and I've talked with Albert and they said "just wait," so that's what we did. I decided to shoot an on-camera diary of myself talking to the camera and tracking our "Waiting for Godot" situation. We'd gone and shot pick-up shots of every place we could think of, and we'd just sit there and wait.

Taylor, partially out of frustration, his documentary background, and a crew just standing by, naturally started to document on film a daily diary capturing the production's frustration of waiting for Chuck.

TH: (FROM THE FILM *DIARY, DAY THREE*) "We miss you Chuck. We're waiting. We want very much to make this film, and we hope you'll join us soon. This is scene 136, this is take 1 of 136, but this is our third day of the diary. We are here at the hotel. This is the crew behind me. This is the third day of these installments. This morning we were supposed to go out to Chuck Berry's old neighborhood and talk with him about his life, his early life, his family. We were going to go to his sister's house, where his father, who is about ninety-three years old, lives. He's talked a lot about his father and we wanted to get the father and I think he wanted to get the father in the film. But this morning I got a phone call from Chuck saying he was not going to be able to come today. He was ill, and, that may very well be so. So this has now happened with a fair degree of regularity and he hasn't been ill. But he could very well be sick today, and if so, it's certainly understandable he can't work, but we are again all here. We are hoping to be able to get things in the film that we think are important to him, and it's getting increasingly frustrating that we've come all this way and money is being spent. At the same time, it seems as though things that he's agreed to, things that we talked about doing with him, he's changed his mind. Second of all, he's asked the producer and the associate producer to go out and negotiate again today with Chuck, so they're on their way."

Inevitably the thing about filming when someone's not cooperating, well, it takes a long time. Chuck Berry, by the time he got there, I preinterviewed him, he knew, we knew each other. So when he finally came almost what, seven, eight hours after we were there, it turned into a late night, but once I went in and got it, he was fantastic. So our first day at the Cosmo Club was very, very cool. So now every day after that turned out to be a replication of the same thing.

SB: I said to Chuck, "what's going on here? Last night I told you that I would pick you up in the morning and you said no problem, so, what's the problem." He said, "the problem is we don't have an agreement for today's shoot," and I said "it is my understanding we did have an agreement." He said "no that was an agreement for yesterday's shoot." He said "you better get your attorney out here," and I said "no. What do you want?" He said "well, you need your attorney" and I said "no what do you want. Just write it up." He said, "well I wouldn't do that if I was you. I mean, I would really advise you to have your attorney here." He would say to me, "this is not in my contract to do this part of the filming. I'm only supposed to do thirty minutes." Because we all saw this as a ninety-minute film, he actually interpreted that as that he was only to be filmed for ninety minutes total. In other words, a one to one shooting ratio for the entire film.

AS: Stephanie would call me in the morning, as I was in St. Louis dealing with all of the paperwork at the hotel and she was out in Berry Park. And every day or two she would call and say, "you've got to get out here, now."

DA: Chuck Berry considers that if he's doing anything for the show, he's working, and rehearsal is not a rehearsal for the show, rehearsal is another work situation.

SP: We needed help in figuring out how to deal with it from just Universal's point of view. Nobody wanted to see Stephanie's business go down the tubes because of this, so we had to figure out a way to deal with something that was a run-away train. No questions about it. But you know what, I don't think anyone, once it was made, regretted it in any way. It didn't make money right away. The theatrical release was small, but everybody is really proud to have been involved in that film. And I can't imagine anybody at Universal being sorry that it's part of the catalog there. So I don't know if it all comes out in the wash from this perspective. I can remember how horrendous it was, I thought my own job was at stake.

AS: We had to pay him to use his Cadillac Eldorado for the film. We had to pay him three hundred dollars for the month. But we had to do an agreement with Chuck to pay him to use his car. Everything was a deal.

TA: Everything with Chuck was about "No Money Down," to reference one of his song titles, "No Money, No Chucky."

AS: This pattern continued on right into postproduction with Chuck. We had to have an agreement for the film dubbing based on how long he would be recording. $5,000 in cash for three hours, forty-five minutes of dubbing and looping. And then there was an additional balance that was due if we went over the time limit we had agreed on.

SB: The need for the lip syncing was partly due to two facts: that he went and did another show in the middle of our filming and partly because Taylor had him doing two concerts.

TA: Chuck had a contract at Universal Pictures that was prenegotiated with Universal and Stephanie and he signed it. But as we learned on this movie, contracts are subject to anyone's interpretation, and Chuck Berry had a very interesting way of interpreting contract clauses on a daily basis.

AS: I think that what was intended initially because nobody figured it was going to be this long and would just be a concert, some interviews with Chuck, became a big thing.

SB: Every time that Taylor said he wanted to do something to expand the film's vision, Chuck happily agreed to it. Then the phone would ring and he would say, hi, Stephanie, guess what, that's not in the deal. After consulting with Universal's lawyers, they advised us each time that Chuck made a new demand for money, to have Chuck write it up himself and later we could claim we were forced to sign under duress. We went to his house and he had this little typewriter, but he sat down and rewrote another amendment for money to be added to the contract.

TA: And then there were the two concerts the night of the show.

AS: I remember that at the time of the show, he wouldn't go on for the second show, because that wasn't in his deal. And then we had to go get $30,000. And I remember walking into his dressing with Stephanie and she threw the bag at his head. It had cash in it. One of the great moments in rock and roll.

TH: How much was Chuck Berry getting paid for this film? Let's see, he was being paid for music rights, and he was being paid to do it. He was a producer as far as I was concerned. His name was on the film.

SB: I think it started at something like $150,000 and ended up at something like $800,000.

TH: He knew he had us by the short and curlys. He knew it, and in this instance he was bound and determined to squeeze every amount of cash he could, and that's what he did over the course of the film. So I started thinking, *what am I going to do.* We went out to Berry Park and we were shooting rehearsals, and it was very cool. And Robert Cray was one of the first people, and I've got a great thing where he's doing "Come On." I got really terrific stuff, exchanges, Eric Clapton shows up, Julian Lennon shows up. Everything is like working. Linda Ronstadt is coming to town. Everything is working okay and then I'm like getting ready to shoot the next day. I've got it all planned out. We're going to go and we're going to meet his father. And I really wanted to get his family in this movie. I thought that was very important. I say, "Chuck, we're going to be doing this the next day. We're going to be here, and here," and he says "oh I can't shoot tomorrow." I said, "you can't shoot tomorrow, what do you mean? I've got five days for this entire schedule. Chuck we've got these things set up." He says, "I can't shoot. I'm going to Columbus, Ohio, I'm performing a gig there." I mean, no one had heard this.

SP: I mean that became a theme throughout the production because he was in a position to sort of hold the production up for cash whenever he wanted to, and that's what happened. I can recall quite a few conversations about that, and, you know, it was hard not to go along because we needed to keep

rolling. And he knew that. And again I think money was
very important to him. The commerce of the music business
was important to him, and that I know because he and every
other black musician in the fifties were ripped-off horribly.
And it probably went on a lot longer with him and a lot of the
black artists more than the white artists as time went on. And
I think he carried that with him all of his life and that's how it
manifested itself. That he was going to control how he got paid
for being Chuck Berry. And I can understand that. He was
more bitter than a lot of people, but he was also smarter than
a lot of people. You know, and he knew exactly how to, ah, get
what he felt he was owed.

AS: It was a moving target, and as different stuff came up we
had to go back to MCA. There were these amendments that
were happening during the production. So we were giving him
more money and we had to go back to Universal MCA to say
"okay Chuck wants this and Chuck wants that." They would
agree and then we had to do an amendment with Chuck.

TH: I talked to Dick Allen. Dick Allen is an important guy
because he started with the Billy Shaw agency representing
and booking a lot of black acts. In his time, he booked and was
close to James Brown. He was close to Solomon Burke. He was
close to Aretha, and, many, many other very big-time black
guys, and every single one of them is focused on the money.
This is something that comes from their process of realizing as
record artists they weren't going to make a lot of money from
their record companies. They knew their record companies
were going to cheat them, or pay them very low royalties.
Where they made their money was on the road. And when
they made their money, it was in cash, and to be paid every
night. And everything that Dick Allen ever told me about

James Brown, well, it made Chuck Berry look like a piker. He wanted to see the money.

DA: He's a marvelous artist. I mean he stayed a star all these years because he's incredible. And his songs are great. He's a wonderful entertainer. He has a rapport with the audience that they get the second he walks on the stage, even those people who have never seen him before. And when he goes out there to perform, and does it, the guy is incredible. But then he'll hurt himself in order to save a dollar or cost somebody else a dollar. And, in my mind, he should put more thought to his legacy because he should have the greatest legacy.

SB: There are some people who have an obsession and maybe it's the early deprivation, or realizing the importance, or having his music stolen from him initially, that and seeing also the Beatles and the Stones really get the accolades that he never really got in the same way. They got it by mimicking him, by taking his music and reworking it. But he never, you know, he was never at Shea Stadium like The Beatles were. Ah, he was never in those huge venues. There was never a Chuck Berrymania.

CHAPTER FOUR
Checking Out Chuck's Performance

So, WE WERE GOING to go into business with the legendary Chuck Berry, but, what was he like these days as a performer? He was pushing sixty. Could he still wow the crowds with "Johnny B. Goode" and "Maybelline"? We found out that he was booked to do another of his drop-in and drop-out road gigs. This time at The United Center in Chicago during halftime at a Chicago Bulls basketball game.

TOM ADELMAN: So Stephanie sends me to Chicago to see Chuck Berry play. Someone needed to see what he was like on stage. Chuck Berry picks me up at the airport in his Cherry Red Cadillac, green cap, and green plaid jacket, and I put my luggage in the back seat and sit in the passenger seat, and he drives us to the United Center. It was a night game and was getting close to game time. All Chuck carried with him was his Gibson electric guitar. So I carried the guitar, went into the United Center and everyone recognizes Chuck Berry, and they bring him right to his dressing room. We sit in the dressing room, he has a sandwich or something and then someone escorts us up to our seats for the game, which were the first seats in the first row, right under one of the baskets. We see the players warming up, and I think that was my first time ever seeing a young Michael Jordan. I didn't really know who he was, but there he was, #23, and we're sitting there. Gregory Hines and Billy Crystal walk over, and Gregory says,

"Chuck I just wanted to say hello. I'm Gregory Hines and this is Billy Crystal and we are huge, huge fans of you and your music. It's an honor to meet you." They were fairly well-known celebrities at that time. Chuck did not even make eye contact with them. He just kept looking straight ahead at the players warming up, didn't say a word, and I looked up at Billy Crystal and Gregory Hines and they looked at each other, and I just like kind of shrugged my shoulders, and, hey guys, I don't know. And, they walked away. So then the basketball game starts and we're watching the game, and when it's about six minutes or seven minutes left in the second quarter, someone comes over and escorts Chuck and me back down to his dressing room. There is no wardrobe change. He's just going to play in what he came dressed in. There's a knock on the door and the band comes in, the backup band that Chuck was going to use that night. These backup bands on the road, well, everybody knows Chuck Berry's repertoire and they are just young guys in their twenties, all excited to be backing up the father of rock and roll. And "Chuck it's an honor to be playing with you tonight. What do you want to play tonight," and he just looked at them. He didn't answer right away and then responded. I think he might have said something like get out of my dressing room. Poor guys all looked deflated and just left the dressing room. Its halftime at the basketball game and someone comes down and gets us. Chuck Berry gets up on stage, the band is already there, and he must have played about five or six numbers and blew the house down. I couldn't believe it. Part of it was the excitement of just being right there up close and personal and seeing Chuck Berry. I had seen a lot of great concerts in my day, The Beatles, The Stones, but this was different. This guy was unbelievable…it was the music and his stage charisma and the audience response. The show is over,

Chuck leaves the stage and that's it. We're not watching the rest of the basketball game. We get back into his car, he looks at me and says, "what do you want to do now?" Did this mean I was going to party with Chuck Berry on a Saturday night? Wow. There is this very close friend of mine who I grew up with, a great, great soul singer, harpist, and blues musician, then and now, named Tad Robinson, who lives in Indiana. I told him I was coming to that part of the world, Chicago. He told me about this up and coming blues guitar player and singer-songwriter named Robert Cray. Tad said, "you and Chuck must check him out." So, I said, "Chuck I hear there's this incredible musician named Robert Cray who is playing at the Cubby Bear, which is a famous Chicago joint right across the street from Wrigley Field." And I said we could go see him. Chuck said, "yeah let's do that." So Chuck, of course, knows where it is, and he drives us toward the Cubby Bear. There's not a lot of cars on the street at this point…it's probably around eleven o'clock at night. I think it was a Saturday night, or a Friday night, he turns down this street that's one-way and he's driving in the wrong direction. All of a sudden we see flashing lights behind us and he pulls over. The police get out and see it's Chuck Berry, and he and I get out of the car. One of the policemen say, "Chuck, hey good to see you again. You know you're going down a one-way street the wrong way." Chuck opens up the trunk of the car, and he's got a stack of his albums in there and hands two of them to the cops. The cops took the albums and let him off without a ticket. We get back in the car, turn around going in the right direction, and end up at the Cubby Bear. We're parked about a few car spots away from the entrance to the Club. There's a line up and you hear music blasting from inside. And there must be thirty or forty people in line waiting to get in. I start walking toward the front of the line by the entrance, turn around and see Chuck Berry walking fast across the railroad tracks heading toward a McDonalds. I said, "Chuck, where are you going?" He doesn't even respond, so I follow him across those tracks into McDonald's. There's only the people working behind the counter and maybe one or two people sitting at a table somewhere. It was a very empty joint. Chuck Berry walked over to the counter and the two McDonald employees know who he is, of course, but they don't say anything. He says "let me have two Big Macs, two orange juices and two hot apple pies." We're going to have dinner and he orders for me. Never asked me what I would like, he just ordered. He gets the food on one of those orange plastic trays, and we go way to the side to those colored plastic tables and round chairs that you sit in that swivel. Chuck sits down, places the tray down and he sticks a Big Mac, a hot apple pie, an orange juice, and one paper napkin in front of me and starts to eat his dinner. We still haven't said a word to each other. We're sitting there, and I'm eating my burger, and he's eating his burger and taking sips of the orange juice through a straw and he's just like looking at me, and he doesn't take his eyes off of me. He's just staring at me and so, I'm just staring at him and taking bites of my burger. And I'm very intimidated and careful about what I say. Don't say anything that's going to like fuck this up and maybe blow up the whole show. And I just said, "that's a hell of a beautiful airport, Lambert, that you got there." He said something like, "I've been in all of them...been in them all. Been in every airport in the world," and that was it, that was the end of the conversation. We finished our meal, get up, and walk over to the Cubby Bear. We walk right to the front entrance and the guy at the door stops us and says, "that's five dollars each please." Chuck Berry looks at him and says, "Chuck Berry doesn't pay to go into this shithole." "I'm sorry, I know who you are but everybody has to pay to get in, sir." I said, "Chuck, no problem, it's okay." I pull out ten bucks and said "sir, it's okay." He stamps my wrist and I turn around and Chuck's not there. I see him walking away fast. He's gets in his car and I'm trying to catch up to him, but, he pulls away and leaves with all my luggage in the car. And that was it, he was gone. And I'm left there with, I think maybe ten to fifteen dollars in my pocket, nothing else, and so I go into the Cubby Bear. At that point, Robert Cray's on stage and it was truly unbelievable how hot this guy was. It was a smoke-filled room, you know, the blues and his voice and just his charisma were just flying off the stage. I said to myself, this guy's unbelievable, a star. And, I had never heard of him. After the show, I walked over to Robert Cray, and said "I'm here representing Delilah Films, and we're going to do this Chuck Berry movie, and Keith Richards is going to be the music director and Taylor Hackford is directing. It's a celebration of Chuck's sixtieth birthday. Is this something you'd be interested in?" Robert Cray said "absolutely," and he gave me his phone number and his address and his manager's number. After the show, someone gave me a lift to my hotel, and my luggage had been left there. I flew back the next day and told Stephanie about how great Chuck was and about Robert Cray. At the future meeting at Berry Park in Wentzville, Missouri, with Keith, I told him about Robert Cray and I think he may have heard of him. Robert ended up being a vital part of the show performing "Brown Eyed Handsome Man" on stage and playing rhythm guitar on some other numbers. He then went on a worldwide tour with Eric Clapton.

CHAPTER FIVE
Meeting Chuck on his Home Turf

LINE PRODUCER TOM ADELMAN *and I went to visit Chuck at his home, Berry Park, in Wentzville, Missouri. We had no idea what to expect. After all, Chuck was a huge rock star, still performing almost every week. We imagined a huge mansion with all of the trimmings of rock and roll stardom. When we arrived at the St. Louis airport on our first trip, Chuck was there in one of his twelve Cadillacs to pick us up. It was a rainy Sunday. He insisted on going to the DMV to renew his license as our first stop, though we kept saying it must be closed, it being Sunday. But, for Chuck, maybe they would open it. There was nobody there to open it, of course.*

TOM ADELMAN: This was our first experience together alone with Chuck Berry. And Stephanie and I are sitting there in this Cadillac, which thank God was not an open convertible, as it was raining. And he is at the top of the steps leading to the doors of city hall and knocking, and knocking. But as Stephanie said, this was a Sunday and city hall was closed. Stephanie and I looked at each other perplexed, "What is he doing?" After a few minutes, Chuck came back down and got into the driver's seat and said, "I think they are closed." Welcome to the Chuck Berry Show.

STEPHANIE BENNETT: Onward to Berry Park, down Chuck's version of Highway 61, in a serious thunder storm. As we drove in the pouring rain to Chuck's house, suddenly, in the middle of the highway, he stopped the car and ran across six lanes of traffic, carrying a gas can. We were panicking, thinking: "There goes our star, he's going to get killed."

TA: Chuck is zigzagging through oncoming traffic in both directions, and I turned to Stephanie and asked her if we happened to have cast insurance in place yet for the movie, as our star is about to get whacked by a forty-foot semi?

SB: There was no insurance in place yet, and so we hoped for the best. He disappeared over the hill and we could see the faint neon sign of an Esso station glowing in the haze. After a few minutes, we saw this silhouette of a figure appear from over the hill.

TA: And there he was, heading down this slippery slope (the first of many by the way) and ready to maneuver back across the busy highway to the Cadillac. We both kind of said a prayer to the Gods of rock and roll to let Chuck make it through the night, as John Lennon once sang.

SB: Chuck ran back and filled the car with gas, and we proceeded to go to a restaurant to have what he described as the best ribs in town. This was debatable.

TA: Chuck stops at this little rib place on the outskirts of St. Louis and leads us into the place. There is a jukebox. Chuck ordered lunch for all three of us. He then went over to the jukebox and selected a cut by Louis Jordan. He then joined us at the table and said, "You are both in for a real St. Louis treat." He was smiling with that kind of Cheshire cat grin that we eventually came to see as a signal that something unexpected was about to happen.

SB: This server whom Chuck clearly knew came out with three plates of Missouri ribs and beans and laid them out for us to carve into. The only problem was that they were 90 percent fat. Tom and I looked at each other in stomach shock, but we had to partake, as not to insult our "star." Meanwhile, Chuck is downing the ribs at full rock and roll speed. And so, we ate.

TA: The rest of the story in terms of what happened to each of us later that night at the hotel, well, let's just leave that to your imaginations, but it wasn't pretty.

SB: Finally, arriving at Berry Park, we were shocked to see a run-down house. In the living room there were two big TV screens. One was playing scenes from Auschwitz. On the other was the Playboy Channel. Was he trying to shock us? He ultimately kept them on during the whole time we were filming at his house, much to the amazement of everyone on the crew. And both shows must have been on some kind of a loop because that was all he ever played. But before any filming took place there would be several more scouting and "getting to know you" bonding trips. They took place in St. Louis, at Chuck's house Berry Park in Wentzville, Mo, at Algoa State Prison in Missouri, in Chicago, and at Keith Richard's house in Jamaica. Of course, it didn't matter where we were, everything went wrong.

CHAPTER SIX
Finding a Director

THE ORIGINS AND SEEDS *of producing a movie about Chuck Berry sprung from a show that I had produced in London through Delilah Films for Cinemax. This was* The Carl Perkins Special: A Rockabilly Session. *This show starred George Harrison, Ringo Star, Eric Clapton, Rosanne Cash and Carl of course, plus others. David Edmunds was the musical director. I actually came up with the concept for this and other later shows, like the* Roy Orbison: A Black and White Night. *These productions, in my opinion, gave rise to MTV's* Unplugged *series which hit the air soon after. But the birth of the* Hail! Hail! Rock 'N' Roll *movie and the effort to identify the right director came to life like this:*

TOM ADELMAN: Stephanie, tell me about the origins of how you came up with the idea and concept of doing something on Chuck Berry.

STEPHANIE BENNETT: After we did the Carl Perkins show, we were thinking of what other legends we could do. I pitched the idea to Betty Bitterman of Home Box Office who liked the idea of Chuck Berry. After your trip to see Chuck in Chicago, we went to The Lone Star Café on Fifth Avenue in the Village and we saw Chuck play there. It was a very small place. He was amazing, and so Betty was committed to doing it, and then we started talking about directors.

TA: At first, we were talking about a television production if I remember correctly?

SB: I think you and I started having a discussion saying that Chuck Berry deserved something more grand, maybe it should be a feature. I hadn't signed a deal with Betty at that point, and she was still kind of hemming and hawing a bit about it. You know it would sort of depend on who the musical guests were going to be. That was her whole thing. So, I think that you and I came up with this idea that if we could get a big-name director, that person could help attract big name musical talent. And so, we came up with a list of people and I remember they were Barry Levinson, Bob Rafelson…

TA: Richard Tuggle.

SB: And Taylor Hackford.

TA: And there was one more, Milos Foreman.

SB: So we set it up interviews, meeting with all of the director candidates, some of them with Chuck.

TA: You and I went with Chuck Berry to a hotel on Sunset Blvd, where Barry Levinson was staying. We went up to his room, and Chuck was sitting in an armchair and Barry Levinson was talking to him, but was kind of kneeling down in front of him, almost with reverence of Chuck and talking to him about his vision for the movie. I think that he had committed to another project. In the end, as was with all the directors with whom we met, with the exception of Taylor Hackford, Chuck would look at you and say, "that's not my director." Then we set up an introduction for Chuck with Bob Rafelson, who of course was a famous director who had directed The Monkees' *Head* and many other movies including *The Postman Always Rings Twice*. We set up a meeting at a swanky Hollywood staple called Le Dome, which was on Sunset Blvd. Bob Rafelson and his assistant at the time made a reservation at the largest round table at Le Dome. Clearly Rafelson knew management, and so he must have been there all the time, probably conducting meetings. Stephanie and I arrive, and Bob was there with his assistant. We all sit down and are waiting for Chuck. Finally, after a bit of time, Chuck Berry walked in and Bob gets up and introduces himself to Chuck. Chuck sits down and has a brown paper bag with him. There was a little bit of getting-to-know-you talk between Chuck and Bob Rafelson. And then the waiter comes over with the menus, and Bob orders a bottle of very fine wine. So everybody looked at their menu, except Chuck, who instead opens up his brown paper bag and pulls out a McDonald's Big Mac, fries, an orange juice, and a hot apple pie. I remember Rafelson looking at him and saying, "Chuck, you know, please, you're my guest. Please order whatever you want." And Chuck turns to Rafelson and says, "Nobody tells Chuck Berry what to eat." And so, we sat there and Chuck Berry ate a McDonald's cheeseburger with French fries, while Bob Rafelson dined on sirloin steak and everybody else had normal meals from Le Dome, and that was the Bob Rafelson meeting with Chuck Berry. I think Stephanie and I ordered burgers so as to make Chuck feel a bit more comfortable. But, I don't remember if Le Dome had any orange juice or hot apple pie on the menu that evening.

Next came director Richard Tuggle, who had directed Escape From Alcatraz *starring Clint Eastwood.*

TA: Stephanie and I were staying at the Sunset Marquis. She had a rental car and we drove down to Richard Tuggle's set, which was at a house off of the Venice boardwalk where he was shooting a movie. We talked with Richard Tuggle who was a nice guy, but I don't think either of us thought it would be a good fit with Chuck.

SB: I think you and I decided, even though Richard was anxious to do it, and we both liked him a lot, that a meeting with Chuck would not be productive. By that point we kind of could read what type of personality might relate to Chuck, and those choices were clearly becoming few and far between. Then you went to see Milos Forman on your own.

TA: Yes, Milos Forman, the great Polish director who did an American film *Hair*, which was the great sixties musical that documented the hippie movement. And, of course, later on he directed the wonderful film *Amadeus* about Mozart. Milos clearly was attracted to musical content in film. Anyway, Forman was living in a penthouse apartment on Central Park South in New York City, just west of the Plaza Hotel. We had been informed that Milos was interested in this, and everybody's eyes lit up and, well, this guy was a legendary director. He wanted us to send him a package of research and materials that he could review prior to any meeting with Chuck Berry. Delilah Films had an office in New York City at that time, even though we relocated the company to Hollywood for the making of the movie. We put together a box of research, which included all of the video tapes of Chuck performing that we could find, which in those days were on VHS or ¾ inch tape, plus books, cassettes, and vinyl records of Chuck's music, and everything you could possibly imagine relating to Chuck Berry went into this big brown cardboard box. So, Stephanie asked me to jump into a taxi and take this stuff up to where he was staying and give it to Milos. I take a taxi up to the building, holding this big box, which was heavy and the doorman said, "who are you going to see?" I told him and I was given access to this private elevator which went straight up to the penthouse. I knock on the door and there's no answer. The big box I'm holding was getting heavier by the minute and I knocked again and finally I hear this voice, "What?" And I said, "this is Tom Adelman from Delilah Films with research material for Mr. Forman." The door is unlocked, swings open, and there is Milos Forman in this red velvet smoking jacket. He looked like one of those guys, like Hugh Hefner wearing one of those velvet smoking jackets. I said, "good morning, Mr. Forman, I'm Tom Adelman from Delilah Films with your package of materials on Chuck Berry." Forman just said "what's that, you got the box?" And I said, "yes, I've got the box right here." And Forman looks at the box, which was now getting really heavy. "Give me the box." I hand over the box and said, "I think you'll find in there all of the video and research material that will be helpful, and if there is anything further that you need, we…" and with that, midsentence, he slammed the door in my face. And that was the end of my experience with Milos Forman. I went down the private lift and hailed a taxi to go back to the Delilah Films office in the West Village. When I walked back into the office, Stephanie said, "so, how did it go" and I think I said something like, "I think he liked me." But then as you recall, Stephanie, Milos wanted to do the movie, but made a very courageous decision. He said that "I would love to do this and I think it could be very compelling and intriguing. And, what a character Chuck is," but then Milos Forman said, "I'm not the right guy. You need somebody who understands the roots of this music and where it came from and that probably needs to be an American director, who understands the history of rhythm and blues and soul and what evolved eventually into Chuck Berry's voice."

SB: Do you recall how we came to Taylor Hackford?

TA: Yes, someone had told me about Lisa Day, who was an editor, and I called her. She had done the Talking Heads film *Stop Making Sense*, as well as Hal Ashby's Rolling Stones film, *Let's Spend the Night Together*. It was obvious that Lisa Day was this red-hot, young, female music performance editor, who seemed to be getting hired to do all the big rock and roll performance films. Lisa Day suggested Taylor Hackford who had directed a rock and roll dramatic feature film called *The Idolmaker*. And Taylor, we found out, understood and really loved music. So we reached out to Taylor's reps and a rendezvous was set up to introduce him and Chuck. Taylor suggested, in quite a contrasting way when compared to Bob Rafelson, who wanted to meet at a high-end restaurant, a less pretentious place to meet. Taylor chose this rundown Hollywood Chinese restaurant that he was comfortable in and he knew that Chuck would be comfortable in.

TAYLOR HACKFORD: Well, you have to understand that I had met Chuck there several years before. I suggested the Sun Palace because I knew he knew the restaurant. The Sun Palace was on Vine across from the Palace nightclub. Years before I was in there with my son Rio, who was a little boy, and I looked over at a booth, and there was Chuck, sitting all alone eating Chinese food, completely by himself. And I saw him and I knew who he was, and I went over because Rio was pretty hip to music…he was only about six or seven, but I played Chuck for him a lot. So I said, "Rio, that's Chuck Berry, do you want to get his autograph?" Well, in truth, I really wanted to get it, and Rio said yes, and so we went over to his table and I said, "Mr. Berry, my son is a big lover of your music, as I am, and I'd love to get your autograph for him." He was very cool, he wrote it down on a napkin and he gave it to us. That was probably five years before Delilah called. And so, I suggested the Sun Palace because I knew Chuck knew it and liked it.

SB: It's interesting because when you have dinner with Taylor, he always takes you to these authentic places. He would never go to Le Dome, that's for sure. I have never been to a restaurant with him that wasn't some really kind of working man's restaurant. And so, I'm not surprised he chose that restaurant.

TA: We all rendezvous at The Sun Palace Chinese restaurant in Hollywood. Chuck shows up this time without a brown McDonald's bag.

SB: I remember that Taylor really engaged Chuck. I mean they got along. I remember after that Chuck gave his approval on Taylor and said, "that's the guy." Well, we realized that that was the guy too.

TA: I kind of remember the conversation a little bit also where Taylor was talking about his life and about Chuck's music and why he was interested in telling the story. At that meeting Taylor said "Chuck, I would consider this if you come clean about your two experiences going to jail. That's got to be part of story for me to want to do this."

TH: I was well aware of Chuck Berry's peccadilloes, as it were, you know. How difficult he could be, but when you're making a documentary, your biggest enemy is falling into the trap of honoring, especially a celebratory documentary. You know, everyone's saying, "oh, he's so great. Oh, he's so wonderful." It's boring and it's nice, but its boring. And I realized with Chuck Berry there was a good chance that something was going to happen that would be untoward, knowing that he was the original bad boy of rock and roll. I mean, he really was. And that's why I thought that there was a chance with this film to really get something. At the same time, as a former documentary filmmaker, because I cut my teeth on documentaries—that's how I started—I knew if you have someone who's hiding and refuses to cooperate, you can have trouble. So I came prepared and when I sat down with Chuck, I said, "listen, I want to deal with everything. I want to deal with your time in prison. I want to do a whole portrait, because I think this is an important film. I think you're the most important person in rock and roll." I wasn't saying this to butter him up; although, I was hoping he would be pleased. I was saying it, because I truly believe it, I believe he's the most important person in the birth of rock and roll. And so I said this at that initial dinner, you remember Tom because you were there, and so Chuck went fine, "I'm happy to have you. I want you to be on board. And I welcome you and I want to shoot this in St. Louis. It's my home town. I want to go to the Fox Theatre." There are certain things he said he wanted to do at that meeting. And I said "fine." I was just looking for a green light from him to go ahead and be able to have a no-holds-barred Chuck Berry documentary. And, of course, that's what I hoped would happen when we got Wentzville, but, of course, I found that this was not necessarily the case.

TA: I think we all were just so enamored and seduced by Taylor because he was such a regular guy, but understood and spoke about music and was so knowledgeable about the roots of Chuck's music, and everybody who had influenced Chuck. Taylor was an encyclopedia and had a knowledge that clearly made Chuck see that this guy understands him and where he came from, and none of those other directors he thought did. Taylor was just so down-to-earth and understood music, and that's why Chuck felt comfortable with him. And so did

Stephanie and so did I. I remember you and I left and said, "brilliant, this is the guy." We were very excited, because we liked Taylor.

SB: Yes, he was not Hollywood stuck-up or a nose in the air kind of a person. He was a regular guy. I had a relationship with Suzie Peterson at MCA because I had already made some films with her like The Doors: Live in Europe 1968, and another one called Women in Rock. And originally, if you remember, I think we did a budget that was about eight hundred or something thousand dollars. Ultimately it turned out to be 3.5 million dollars. But we didn't know Taylor at that point or Chuck, or what was going to happen in the future. And then we had the whole discussion about who should be the musical director.

CHAPTER SEVEN
Finding a Musical Director

AT THE VERY INCEPTION of the Chuck Berry movie, after Taylor Hackford had been engaged to direct the movie, the first thing that we needed to do was to hire a musical director; someone who understood Chuck's music, his influences and what his body of work meant to the evolution of rock and roll. All of us were huge fans of Martin Scorsese's concert film, The Last Waltz, which documented The Band's final performance as a touring entity. So I had the idea of engaging Robbie Robertson, the lead song writer and guitarist of the group The Band, as a musical director for Hail! Hail! Rock 'N' Roll.

STEPHANIE BENNETT: My husband, Jim Mervis, and I had a musician friend Scott Richardson, and Scott knew Robbie Robertson. It was my idea to come up with a format like *The Last Waltz*, part documentary and part concert. And Robbie Robertson obviously was the guy behind *The Last Waltz*. So, Scott, who is also a musician, set up a meeting with Robbie. Scott, Tom, and I went to meet with Robbie and I explained the concept to him, and that Taylor had signed on as the director, and I talked about my vision for the film. Robbie said he knew who really should do this and that is Keith Richards. He offered to make a phone call to Keith. To our good fortune, it was right at the moment when Mick Jagger, for the first time ever, decided to do a solo album without the Rolling Stones. So Keith, we later found out, was really upset about it…that's another story, and so, he was available.

TOM ADELMAN: Yes, and then you were put in touch with Jane Rose, Keith's manager. I think Robbie Robertson called you back and said "give Jane Rose a call." I think that was the first time there was contact with Jane, and you and Jane Rose, of course, became great friends. She ended up naming her dog Delilah after your company, as I recall.

SB: Yes, I went to meet with Jane at her office

JANE ROSE: You came to me and talked about the possibility of doing this. "Would Keith be interested?"

And then we just talked about it. We had to see if Keith and Chuck could gel. So we planned a meeting in Chicago, and that was the first meeting in the hotel when Chuck came in his RV and parked it outside the hotel. He came up, and I remember the hotel was a new hotel, and Keith and he talked, and then Chuck started reciting poetry. I was blown away by how articulate he was and how he and Keith just got along incredibly well and beautifully. I mean it was really, it was one of those magical moments actually, because, you saw the best of both, intellectually and artistically. This was before they actually decided to work together, before all the friction came out. But I do remember that. It was like yeah, well, this is going to be so much fun.

SB: Little did you know.

JR: Little did I know, yeah, yeah.

SB: It was made clear by Jane that Keith was definitely going to have a clash of control between Chuck and himself, and that Keith had to be in charge of the band, that he had to choose his musicians if he were going to be the musical director. I made it clear that on the music side it was Keith's band and Keith had to decide. In terms of guests, we were hoping he would attract major people, which he did, of course.

TA: Speaking of major people, can I just tell you one quick story, which happened before Keith Richards got involved. And that is when you and I were in Los Angeles and we were staying at the Sunset Marquis. It was 1985 and we started meeting with directors. I was sitting having a drink at the pool at the Sunset Marquis. You were in your room making phone calls, and here comes Little Stevie Van Zandt, who sits in one of those folding chairs right next to me by the pool. I was a huge, huge Bruce Springsteen fan and had just gone to five of the 1984 Born in the USA tour shows. And so, there's Little Stevie. So I kind of nonchalantly get up and go to the house phone, call you up and said, "Stevie Van Zandt's sitting right next to me. Should I talk to them about the show?" And you said, "absolutely." So, I come back from the phone and I say, "Steven how are you. I work with Delilah Films. We're doing a Chuck Berry movie," and he's listening to me and someone walks over and it's Bruce Springsteen. I just couldn't believe it. I said, "hello, Mr. Springsteen, I'm Tom Adelman and I was just telling Steven about the Chuck Berry movie that we are producing. Then you came out and joined us." We're all sitting there, and I just remember Bruce listening as you were doing a little bit of a pitch. He said, "call my manager, John Landau, in New York." So that was our first experience with Bruce Springsteen, then later that same day, I'm sitting by the pool and see Phil Collins walking through the area going to his room. Again, I go to the phone and said, "Stephanie, it's Phil Collins." And you said, "well get to it. What are you calling me for? Go after him." So, I followed Phil Collins into the hallway. He's like got his key out to open up his room, and I introduce myself and told him about the Chuck Berry movie. I think that he said, "that sounds interesting, call my manager." But if

I recall, Stephanie, I think you knew someone involved with Phil Collins?

SB: Roger Forrester

TA: Yes, Roger Forrester. Phil, his wife Jill, you, and I were sitting under a tree, and I think Phil may have had a bottle of wine and so we were all having a glass. You talked to Phil Collins about Chuck Berry and the movie.

SB: Then his manager got pissed off that I spoke with him directly.

TA: And that's why he ended up not doing the show?

SB: Yeah, if it wasn't Roger Forrester, it was somebody else, and he was livid that I had spoken with Phil. When I called him, he said "how dare you." It was another jerk of a manager. He screamed at me, "you don't talk to my artists without talking to me first." And I said, "well, it just happened as we were staying in the same hotel."

TA: But at this point, your main focus was signing up a musical director. So, you and Jane Rose had the initial conversation about signing Keith Richards to be the musical director. What happened next after you had said, "of course, Keith will be in charge of the music and pick the band?"

SB: The next hassle was that Chuck wanted us to meet in…

TA: At Berry Park in Wentzville, Missouri. Keith as I recall got right into putting the band together, the musical concept, and bouncing ideas off of Chuck, who more or less sat there listening and taking it all in. Keith asked him about Johnnie Johnson, and could we find him and get him back onto the piano for the rehearsals and the show?

We found out that Johnnie Johnson was indeed in the St. Louis area, working his day job driving a public bus. I had to buy Johnnie a new set of teeth before he would appear on camera at the upcoming concert.

TA: This is the meeting where I first told Keith about Robert Cray who I think already may had heard about him. Keith continued putting the band together: Joey Spampinato from NRBQ on bass, Steve Jordan on drums, Chuck Leavell on Keyboards, etc. Keith had a vision of putting together a super band that would finally serve up Chuck's musical pedigree in the way it deserved to be heard. I specifically recall all of us sitting there and Chuck has one of his many television sets on, and some music show is on, and, bingo, there are The Rolling Stones on TV. Every time this team got together, surreal moments like that occurred, just about all of the time.

SB: Despite Keith's chatting all of us up about what a terrific band he was pulling together to back up Chuck, Chuck had other ideas about who he wanted, which he confided in to me. But, I dared not say anything to Keith or Jane or certain hell would break out, and this was just the beginning.

TA: Chuck says, "we're all going out to my club," so we pile into two cars. There's Keith Richards, Taylor Hackford, Jane Rose, Stephanie Bennett, Michael Frondelli, and myself. Chuck pulls into this parking lot, and we see his club, and music is coming from inside. We walk in and there's a three-piece band on stage. They immediately see Keith Richards and break into a Rolling Stones song. Maybe it was "Honky Tonk Woman" or "Jumpin' Jack Flash." Chuck Berry looks at Keith Richards and says, "there's your band. That's the band that's backing me up." Keith Richards response was, "that's not the band that's backing you up, Chuck." It started to get a little heated and I then think cooler heads prevailed, and we spent the evening talking and having drinks. There were all these strange painted ladies in the club that were like, that looked like hookers from a Fellini movie. And halfway through the evening Chuck Berry comes over and says, "come here a second, Tom." So I get up and follow him to this table at the other end of the bar, and he sits me down between these two ladies and said, "this is my friend Tom, he's working on the show, you take special care of him, got it?" Chuck walks away and leaves me with them. I think their names may have been Pudding and Daisy. So I remember kind of politely excusing myself from Pudding and Daisy's table, and walking over to Taylor Hackford and saying to Taylor, "Chuck just made me sit down with these two, I think they're hookers." And Taylor said, "Tom, we all have to make our little individual sacrifices for the cause and the good of the show." Of course, I ended up not fulfilling my responsibility that evening. The rest of the evening continued, and Stephanie ran interference between Chuck and Keith trying to get Chuck to soften up about the band that Keith was putting together and it was not going to be these guys.

CHAPTER EIGHT
Chuck and Keith in Chicago

GETTING KEITH RICHARDS AND Chuck Berry together in Jamaica. In the lead-up to shooting the movie, there were numerous preproduction get-togethers with the main team. This was all about getting Chuck, Keith, Taylor, and myself on the same page and comfortable as collaborators. The first real getting-to-know-you get-together happened in Chicago, Illinois. Chuck Berry was slated to perform at the 1986 Chicago Blues Festival, and so we all thought this would be a great time and place to bring Keith and Chuck together to break the ice.

KEITH RICHARDS: I've been so disappointed in Chuck Berry's live performances for years and years, and it's as if he didn't give a damn. And if he made a mistake, he'd blame it on the band. He'd just wing it and got through, and he's got such a powerful personality that he's managed to get away with it. I mean everybody said I'm mad to take on the gig. But, so I ordered the straight jacket, allowed six to eight weeks for delivery and if anybody was going to do it, I wanted it to be me. Not so much as musical director as an S&M director, social and musical director, it's the S&M band you know.

TOM ADELMAN: Chuck performs at the Chicago Blues Festival and near the end of his set, he invited Keith Richards to come out, which he did. The place went crazy. Backstage we met with Willie Dixon and Bo Diddley. So, there we were at the festival and after the show, we all decide to go back to Keith's room at the hotel.

HELEN MIRREN: I remember when we went to see him perform in Chicago, and he was the headliner. After the show, Chuck was getting into his Winnebago and the rest of us were leaving in a limo, and word got out that Keith was there. Taylor and I were at the windows, "Keith, Keith, Keith." And people just were hyperexcited because Keith Richards was there. I would have found that so galling if I had been Chuck, you know, because apart from the fact that Keith was saying, "I owe it all to this guy," the audience doesn't know that. They don't appreciate that. They just want the English, you know, rock star. Not the black originator. And I think that was a microcosm of his whole life. Kind of from the late sixties onward. I think he was a person with great feeling. And actually, I think great tenderness, there was a great tenderness in him. There was a real vulnerability that was covered up by all this other stuff. That's what I always felt.

So, we all get into a limo to go back to the hotel and Chuck gets into his Winnebago and drives back to the hotel, or so we thought.

TA: Chuck had driven his huge Winnebago from Wentsville to Chicago for the festival, and he came late to the festival and nobody could track him down. But finally he did drive up to the festival in that monster of an RV. Anyway, after the show, we all took the limo back to the hotel, and Chuck insisted on driving alone in his Winnebago as usual. Keith has his nice suite and we all go up there, and meanwhile everyone's waiting for Chuck. "Where is Chuck? Missing in action again." Well, it turns out that it was an issue of Chuck not being able to find a place to park the Winnebago. We were waiting for him for hours. At one point, room service comes in with this cart filled with liquor. In that room was the main team. Now Keith had invited a bunch of friends of his in Chicago to swing by, various musicians and people. I don't think it was anyone famous, but people came in and out to say hello to Keith. Meanwhile, Chuck is still out trying to park his Winnebago, and no one knows where he is.

Keith Richards had friends and admirers everywhere, as he had been on the road with the Stones by that point for over twenty odd years. And when he blew into a particular town, he liked to connect with those people that he had formed bonds with from past tours.

TA: As we're sitting there Helen Mirren's movie *Excalibur* comes on TV and Helen's talking about that movie, and I'm sitting in the back next to Keith Richards, who is holding a small body acoustic guitar. Stephanie and Helen are talking and someone else is talking to this one and there's music playing and the soundtrack from the movie is colliding with that music, and it's a party. Keith Richards starts playing a Hoagy Carmichael's song, "The Nearness of You." He sings softly and is almost drowned out by the rest of the party going on. I'm sitting right beside him, and basically, only I could hear him, and he's looking at me and he's playing this song to me. Keith Richards is serenading me alone with this song. Wow, this is a moment I'll never forget, And he goes through the first verse, and then everyone in the room starts realizing Keith Richards is singing and so things quiet down and he finishes. Years later Keith Richards recorded "The Nearness of You," and he also performed it with the Rolling Stones on tour. It's obvious he cared about beautiful standards. And I think, if you recall, Stephanie, eventually Chuck Berry showed up after finally finding a place to park the Winnebago. Chuck walks in and sits down next to Keith. We were sitting there watching, and Chuck takes the guitar from Keith and starts doing "Cottage For Sale."

STEPHANIE BENNETT: Yeah, which ended up in the film. I don't think it's a moment any of us ever forgot.

HM: I'll never forget him sitting and playing "A Cottage For Sale." It was just him on the guitar, and he just played the music and sang, and it was the most beautiful, moving, sweet, delicate sort of performance. It was just lovely. And then it was like I always felt that with Chuck that there was a dreamscape, if you like, that he always seemed to have a dream of how he would have loved his life to be, but it was never going to be like that because he was a black guy from where he was from.

Helen Mirren has a way of cutting through to the heart and soul of human behavior, evident, of course, in her acting work and clearly visible in her analysis of Chuck Berry. The next night, we went on a junket to the famous Checkerboard Lounge Bar on the south side of Chicago. Now this was a surreal kind of evening. Here's how Tom remembers it:

TA: Taylor, Helen Mirren, Jane Rose and Keith Richards, and Stephanie and I got into a rented limo to go to the Checkerboard Lounge, a famous club on the south side of Chicago. The Rolling Stones' "Paint It Black" comes on the radio. I remember sitting there in a jump seat listening to the song and looking at Keith Richards listening to the song. This was such a surreal moment, and then Keith started talking about Brian Jones and how tough Brian was to deal with when the band was on the road in those early days. He said the guy was a great musician, but on the road, he would drive everyone nuts. We get to the Checkerboard Lounge and performing was Dr. John. We walk in with Keith Richards and Chuck Berry…the place is packed and, you know, everybody sees it's Chuck Berry, who's probably been there many times, but Keith Richards is the one who gets all the attention. We sit down at a table just off stage right. Keith Richards goes over to the bar and the bartender pulls out a half-empty bottle of Jack Daniels and says, "hey, Keith, I still got it" and he hands him the bottle of Jack, a bottle that Keith had obviously started years before. Keith brings it to the table and we're all watching Dr. John. Then Chuck Berry got up and jammed with him, but Keith didn't. Keith was sitting there and listening to them jam, and the crowd was totally enjoying the moment, and looking at Keith Richards more than Chuck. And that was a memorable night.

CHAPTER NINE
A Scout to Chuck's Prison

CHUCK WENT TO PRISON *several times during his life. When he was eighteen he was sentenced to three years for stealing a car and holding up a store, which he always denied. During this time, for even the most minor of offenses, a black man, especially a poor black man in the South, had no chance of escaping prison time. It was usually substantially more prison time than any white man. Chuck was sentenced to a prison named Algoa in rural Missouri. Director Taylor Hackford and I knew this experience had to have had a considerable impact on his life and wanted to include it in the film. A small group of the production team headed out to scout the location. What was anticipated to be a productive, easy, and informative day turned into anything but. Each person had a different view of what happened, being in different places in the Prison at the time, so the story is told à la Rashomon.*

STEPHANIE BENNETT: Taylor, when you had that first meeting with him, I remember you laid down certain things you wanted to include in the film, and he was not going to hold anything back. One of them, of course, was his prison experience. Did you really believe that at the time, that you would get it all?

TAYLOR HACKFORD: I did believe it, number one, because I really had stated it was important, and number two, I think he was going to deliver on it when we were in Wentzville, because remember, it was in preproduction, and I said, "Chuck remember, I want to go up to the prison." He said "yeah, yeah, I performed up there." Everybody knows Chuck Berry did time in prison. It's an important part of his legend as a true outlaw. They know the creators of rock and roll were always supposed to be the outlaws. Well, Chuck Berry's got the real mug shot to prove it. Most people think that he only went to prison once. That was for the Mann Act, taking an underage girl across the state lines for illicit purposes in the late fifties, but in reality Chuck Berry went to prison as a teenager. He and a group of friends from St. Louis stole a car and were going to drive to California. I mean, a crazy, teenage stunt. Maybe if you were the son of an Alderman or a businessman, a white guy in St. Louis, they would have slapped you on the wrist. Chuck Berry got three years in prison. While he was in prison, Algoa State Prison in Missouri, he developed a lot of, I think, things that were important to him later. You know there was a gospel group he told me that he joined, and they were able to sing and travel outside of prison to various organizations, which gave him an opportunity to kind of ease his time there. I think he read a lot of poetry in prison, and he recites some of those poems that he learned in prison, which is pretty incredible when you realize what a lyricist this man is and why he's different as an artist than many of the other originators of rock and roll. But I wanted to go to Algoa State Prison because I thought it would be an opportunity to really deal with something that people didn't know and also to kind of clarify who this man really is, and Chuck didn't seem against it. He said, "I'm part of their program. I go in there, I do concerts. I try to give a positive image to these guys." He had feelings for them. I called the State Head of Prisons. He said, "yeah, Chuck's part of our program. We love him. He comes in and does stuff." I think I was going to be able to work it out and we could shoot there. So we went on a scout early so that we could actually check it out and know what problems we were going to have. Little did we know then the problems that we would have. I drove to the prison with Stephanie Bennett, the producer; Jerry Lawrenson, my assistant; and Mike Frondelli, the engineer that was going to do the recording. In case we were going to shoot any concerts there, he would be able to check out the situation. We get there. Of course, Chuck is late. He was late oftentimes. The state film commissioner who was there had to leave. So we're waiting. We did have permission to go into the prison. Finally, Chuck pulls up and he's got his daughter and he's got his girlfriend Yvonne. Yvonne's wearing a miniskirt. Stephanie Bennett and Jerry Lawrenson are wearing pants. I can't remember if his daughter was wearing a dress or not. But this miniskirt was very high, right up near the danger zone. And Chuck waves to the guard and says open the gate. The guy says, "hi, Chuck." Opens the gate and we drive up into the prison. Now I've been to prisons before. There is a lot of security that goes on when you go to prison, but this time, there was completely nil. We just drove right up onto the main yard of the prison. And got out of the car. We're standing and a woman guard comes across kind of confused. "What's going on?" We say we have permission. We mention the head of the prison. She said she's going to check it out. She gets on her radio but inmates start coming out of the yard. They saw Chuck. "Hey, Chuck." It was like an old home week at a reunion and he was very warm and friendly with them. And they all came and they crowded around and they said, "you want to see the dormitory" and he said, "yeah, sure," and he left, leaving us there with this woman guard and she seemed quite nervous. She said, "listen I think we should work our way across the yard and go into the Administration Building," so we started to move. Now I had Chuck Berry's video camera. He always carried a video camera every place he went. I said, "Chuck, give me your camera." I started documenting this moment. And we walked across the yard. I was always back. The group was walking, but more inmates started to pour out into the yard, a lot of them, because they heard that Chuck was here. The pied-piper right?

SB: We go to the jail. It was actually a maximum-security jail. These people were there for things like murder, and so we get in the car. On the way Chuck says, "we're going to make a stop." We go to the hospital and he picked up his youngest daughter. So now there's Taylor, Jerry, Yvonne, and myself, and we set off to the prison. Afterward we find out that his daughter had been in a mental institution, which kind of compounds my whole feeling about the fact that he was bipolar. I remember seeing you, Taylor, filming, and I seeing all these people walking around the courtyard, and there was a moment when it was as if they suddenly realized that there were women in the group. We suddenly realized that there were about a thousand prisoners, and we were in the middle of this yard. I don't remember seeing any guards at that point, which is very strange. What happened is that, at the same time I think we realized, "holy shit, we're in a prison, and we are basically completely vulnerable," so we started running. They caught up with us and two of these prisoners grabbed me. One had one arm and another had the other arm, and there was a hand on my crotch, and literally I felt like I was being tugged apart by these two men. At the same time, Yvonne was on the ground and she was wearing a skirt. I thought, thank goodness I was wearing jeans and Jerry was wearing jeans. And they got Yvonne on the ground, and had a boob and pulled her pants down, her underwear off. And the next thing these guards had come up with batons, and they were smashing these prisoners literally to get them to stop holding, stop their grip on us, and I remember the guard, a woman I think, coming and smashing the baton onto, onto these guys. And I was quite severely bruised afterward. The guards guided us into this kitchen, and these guys are rioting. They're hammering on the windows and we're in there and Chuck's in there. And remember we are with his daughter, who's just also been attacked, his daughter who had just come from a mental hospital. And we were really concerned about her, and she said to us, "this is nothing compared to what I've just been through at the hospital," where she said she was attacked. And Taylor turns to Chuck and says, "Chuck what the hell are you doing!?" And he said, "well, I know what it's like for prisoners who've been in jail without seeing a woman, so I figured I'd give them a treat."

MICHAEL FRONDELLI: Poor Stephanie she was just traumatized by this, because she had no idea what to expect. We were crossing this courtyard and the women that were with us were getting groped, pushed down to the ground. They were crying, it was terrifying, and at the same time, I could understand that these guys had been caged for a while.

TH: My problem was letting Chuck handle the arrangements… let's face it, he did drive us up to the Missouri State Penitentiary. He did try to get us in. He, in fact, got us in, and so he did deliver on…the fact that I wanted to go back there to shoot later, that I'm not sure Chuck understood. Chuck, as you well know, Chuck the cash register was always running late, so we were there early. He thought "well, I'm on the clock, and

I gave you this amount of time and I'm getting paid for it, so I can take you up to the prison." I did have a video camera, which Chuck let me have, and I shot everything that went on. But then I gave the camera back to Chuck at the end and he never gave it back to me. That would have been stuff we could have used. He said there was nothing on the video. Bull shit. I know that I was getting things. So he took it and never let me have it, but the experience going to prison and seeing Chuck Berry in that environment was amazing. It would have been an incredible part of our film.

SB: The authorities came into the kitchen. The whole place is really going crazy. And they said, "Chuck used to do performances there." They said, "Chuck, you have created a riot here. You have to do something," so I don't know whether he volunteered to perform for them or if they insisted he do it to quiet them. So Chuck got his guitar from the trunk of his car and played for the prisoners.

TOM ADELMAN: I know Taylor was filming. Whatever happened to the video tape he got?

SB: It was Chuck's camera. Chuck said to Taylor, "give me the camera," and he took it with the tape still in it. What happened to it, I have no idea, but of course it was never in the film and we never went back and filmed there again. It was unbelievable; it was terrifying actually. And then you get a phone call from the Governor. I think it was in the newspaper. Didn't you have to go see somebody afterward because they were upset about what happened. I think they complained and said that there was going to be an investigation or something. Of course, they said, "you can never come back again," but who wanted to go back there. Chuck said it was like a payback to these prisoners, because I think he was incarcerated there for almost two years, obviously without any women. So it was a strange Chuck Berry kind of thing to do.

TH: I had shot film in a prison, so I was aware of what it was like to be in prison. They were never threatening to me. They certainly were threatening and feeling you guys up. Those women, I mean, amazing to be taken in there. But I had images of the excitement on those guys faces. I have a different perspective: number one, I made a film in prison. Although I'm very cautious, I know when the real violence happens, and none of these guys were really interested in violence. They were out to have fun. And it wasn't fun for you, but the reality is, I really don't believe that Chuck Berry ever put any of us in a dangerous situation, because I've been in prison. I've seen people stabbed. I know when men get to a sense of rage and they're going to kill. That's not what this was. This was a celebration. Unfortunately, the celebration for you guys is terrifying. My point is there is a fine line here. I can never believe and I never will believe that Chuck Berry took us there with the sense that any of us were going to be harmed. I do think on the other hand, he did kind of think, well tough, it's not the first time they got felt up. And I know he did these guys a lot of good in spite of what he said to me in terms of "I know what it's like to be in," so it's a strange, he's a strange guy.

SB: Well, he did drive us into the middle of the quadrangle if you remember.

TH: Absolutely.

SB: And then he disappeared.

TH: The thing that was interesting, it's not like he was lying. He had gone back to that prison. He had given classes at that prison. He had done concerts at that prison. He should have and could easily have a resentment about being there for three years, but I do believe he truly empathized with those guys. He understood what it was like to be in there, incarcerated and how horrible it is, and this wasn't for us. We already know, because I talked with the warden, he was often times back there, so in a way, we always wonder about Chuck Berry caring about anybody. He did care about those guys.

SB: Yeah, that's great! Why do you think he didn't let you have the tape?

TH: Because he probably looked at it. If you remember we came in and we were on that open field. I started photographing and when those inmates started coming on the field, I was photographing that little guard, woman guard's saying, "I think we better proceed across this field. Don't act panicked, just follow me," and you know I'm an old documentarian, so I felt a dramatic moment coming, and I'm following along behind you guys, and I think that Yvonne was the first one to go down, and then did you go down too?

SB: No, I had one pulling one arm and one the other, and then one on my crotch, basically.

TH: Right, and I am photographing all of this. You know people could have said to me, "oh gee, why didn't you run in and help those women instead of photographing…"

SB: Yeah, well I did think that actually.

TH: You said that to me once. But the reality is I kind of looked at it like "God, this is an amazing experience" and then once we got inside I was filming and you guys were very shaken, very emotional, and I think frightened, because when you're surrounded by, it must have been two hundred or three hundred guys there and you know you got kind of pent-up male energy, it's frightening. And then, if you remember, the only way that we could get out of the place was Chuck would do a concert in the hallway because there were too many inmates out. When we got to the building all the prisoners now were outside and all the inmates you know climbing on the walls, screaming. People were terrified. We got everybody up and into the building. I tried to calm people down, and said, "listen, you know we're safe. Everything is okay." I stayed out and photographed those inmates as they came in the gymnasium, or whatever it is. There was just this, I felt, this fantastic energy and you could call it violence. I didn't feel they were interested in violence. They're violent men. They were excited. They were going to listen to rock and roll. Chuck shows up. He had come from the dormitory, and it was clear now that the warden had been informed of all this, that we were not going to be able to get out to our cars the way we'd come in, because it was filled with inmates. The only way we were going to get out of there was for Chuck to do a concert. There was a band among the prisoners. He got up on stage. We were in the back of the stage, and I got up on stage and filmed him.

MF: You'll see in the shots and the prison band, one guy's got acoustic guitar. Chuck's got a guitar that looks like his, there's a drummer. He gets up on the stage and he's just doing his thing, and Taylor's up on the stage and he's shooting and shooting, whatever he could, but, Chuck decided he was going to put his girlfriend right at the edge of the stage and very conspicuously, and there are kids just like hanging on the edge of the stage, because some of these kids look like they were no more than maybe nineteen or twenty years old. He's doing his duck walk on the stage and the women are literally trembling from this experience of being accosted going across the courtyard. So finally they call in another shift of guards so we can actually leave. They form an armlock column on the side of the stage so we can go underneath the stage into another holding area where they brought our cars up, and we get out. We all get in the cars, stop at the gate as we're leaving, and go on to Lambert airport. Chuck's going off to Wentzville with his crew. Yvonne turns around to us and says, "I never felt so wanted by so many men," and we were all in shock.

TH: Chuck asked for his camera back and I, of course, tried to establish a thing of trust with him, so I gave him back the camera and said, "I want to keep those two tapes." He said, "let me look at them tonight." So this is to answer your question the long way, I think Chuck looked at that footage. If he gave it back to me, I would use it. I think when he saw what happened with Yvonne down on the ground, she's wearing her miniskirt and her legs up, and those guys reaching in, and all of that stuff, plus the fact that when we finally got inside you guys were crying and you were emotional and you were in shock. And then of course, all these guys coming down and flipping out because they were Chuck's guys, they were inmates. I think when he saw that footage, he didn't want it in his film.

SB: Do you remember, Taylor, you were filming him and asked him why he did it, and he said, "I know what its like to be in jail for three years with no pussy."

TH: Yup.

SB: Also remember we picked up his daughter from the mental institution. We were all concerned about her and she said, "this is nothing compared to what I've been through."

TH: Well, I believe that in a mental institution, I believe it. But Chuck, he did say that; when someone says that to you,

you then start to rethink what you've just been through. I don't know what he said to Yvonne. I know that Yvonne was in his car, she was wearing a very, very short miniskirt. If he was concerned about her, concerned knowing where they were going, he should have said, "put on some slacks. Don't be showing your legs like that, because we're going to a place where guys are hungry for women." He never said that to her. He was a diabolical character.

TA: I remember that he gave instructions for the women to wear skirts for that trip. He knew what was going to go down.

SB: It's like an offering, it is diabolical when you think that he was offering us, including his daughter.

TH: I know, I know. And what he did and this is going back to what you said at that dinner, I said to Chuck, "if I do this film, I want to be able to see things that other people haven't. I want to be able to go in, I want to go to the jail, the first place you went to jail." My problem was I should have had my own camera. I should have had my own ability to shoot stuff. I was thinking I was going to research. I wanted to keep my eyes open. Who knew what was going to happen. I was just there, none of this was planned. We didn't have any idea, but what I did have, and I had planned it, and I got permission from the warden that we were coming back on Monday, remember? We had a date to shoot there...our first day and because of what happened, and the anarchy and the near riot that happened, the Warden was pissed and wouldn't let us come back. So I fault myself. I should have had a camera with me.

SB: Yeah, well, it's still a memorable part of filmmaking that's for sure.

TH: It was, and the thing that's a killer is that I don't have the images to go with that story, because it was really amazing. That was like the go-go girls at Whiskey A Go Go where he played a lot.

CHAPTER TEN
Two Nights in Chuck's Missouri Home

WHEN CHUCK HEARD WE were going to be staying in a motel in Wentzville close to Berry Park, he suggested to me that he would build an addition to his house and we could all stay there. I was doubtful, based on the quality of furnishings and the seemingly slapped together house we had seen, that it might not be acceptable. After all, most of us, especially Keith, stayed in four-star hotels. All our other stars like Eric Clapton stayed at the Motel 6 type accommodation. I think they realized there was one big prima donna too many already in the show. However, once again Chuck saw dollar signs and decided to build an addition to his house for the main production team. Tom Adelman and I had only seen the kitchen, the living room, and the club house where he had apparently recorded in the past, so I decided that after it was built I should take a trip and see for myself if it was acceptable. This was a big mistake.

STEPHANIE BENNETT: Chuck picked me up at the airport and he was quite friendly, and I said I was looking forward to seeing what he had built. When we arrived, he took me to the new addition, which was sort of stuck on to the end of the house. He used the cheapest materials and the walls were made of plasterboard, toxic I'm sure. The rooms had beds and bathrooms en suite. I still wondered how I could get Keith Richards to stay here in Chuck's thrown together addition. Jane would be my secret weapon. After getting the grand tour, he suggested that perhaps I might like a jacuzzi. I told him I was allergic to them or some lame excuse, so he turned on his heels and disappeared. It was the evening by then and his assistant who had an office there had left for the day. She lived somewhere on the property in a trailer, though I had no idea where. I wandered through the house calling out "Chuck, Chuck." I hadn't eaten and had planned to go back to New York that night, but how to do it. We were miles away from anywhere and there was a huge gate locked up on the property. You could not get in, but, you could also not get out. Hours go by, I look in the refrigerator for a snack, but there are just sodas. It was dark by now. I was paralyzed with fear, so I decided I would just lay down on one of the beds, wedge something against the door and keep my clothes on. The next day I asked Fran to get me a taxi to the airport. She never mentioned Chuck, and I was happy not to run into him. Of course this was not the end of our little rendezvous. We all did end up staying there for one night. It was furnished very much like his LA house—decorated circa the seventies with fake fur covers on the beds, and as usual Keith made his room look more livable tying scarfs around lamps. The only sweet thing that happened was when I walked into his room, and Keith talked about Mick doing a solo album, something they had sworn to each other no one would do. He said it felt like a divorce. I could only say our luck was that because of this split, he was available for our film. Jane said it was his savior. Something he would never forget. That night we took to our rooms, Taylor and Helen, Keith, Jane Rose, and me. I was relieved that Keith didn't act like a prima donna and agreed to stay there. Of course Chuck charged us. Before going to bed, I felt secure with Taylor and Helen next door. I went to the bathroom to clean my teeth. When I turned the tap on, the water started gushing out of the pipe under the sink! Soon the whole room was flooded. I had no idea what to do (where was Tom when I needed him)! I ran through the house shouting, "Chuck, Chuck—there's a flood." Next thing I know, he and Yvonne, his part-time girlfriend, who lived in a trailer nearby came running into the room with a heavy vacuum. They proceeded to suck up almost all of the water, but then when they went to move the apparatus full of water it exploded. The result was that I spent the night on a lake—at least the bed didn't float, but it was a strange feeling. As the result of Keith agreeing to stay at Chuck's house he demanded, "you come to my house now." After all, it was the Chuck/Keith show.

CHAPTER ELEVEN
A Grand Tour of St. Louis in Chuck's Winnebago

IN ONE OF THE *first times the main production team got together, Chuck Berry invited all of us for a grand tour of some of the hot spots of St. Louis, Missouri, the gateway to the West. I believe this may have been the first, and definitely, the last time that he convinced us all to ride along in his Winnebago, with him behind the wheel.*

TOM ADELMAN: The first day in St. Louis was a grand tour, courtesy of Chuck Berry, who was also the designated driver. We all got into his Winnebago and took off on a little tour of St. Louis. In that Winnebago you have Chuck Berry behind the wheel, and Keith Richards, Taylor Hackford, Stephanie Bennett, Jane Rose, and me. The interior of Chuck's RV was a collage of colors and styles with posters of Playboy Bunnies as the main decorative theme throughout. In fact, there were all kinds of other stuff on the walls, which gave one pause as we were settling into this Chuck Berry Magical Mystery Tour. So, we pull out into traffic with Chuck driving, and after a short distance he pulls over to some neighborhood street across from the Cosmopolitan Club in a predominately black neighborhood. We all heard a scraping or a bang as the Winnebago struck something hard on the right side. When we stopped, a bunch of neighborhood residents are gathering, and there is a commotion. Some local lady starts in. She knows it's Chuck Berry's Winnebago, and so she starts knocking on the window or door and saying, "Chuck Berry you come on out here, I know you're in there, Chuck Berry. I remember what you did last time. Chuck Berry, you come on out. I want to talk to you."

Now, we all knew that Chuck had hit something, but were not quite sure what he had hit.

TA: Chuck Berry turns to me and says, "Tom go out there and fix this problem." I looked at Taylor Hackford and Taylor says, "Tomas, (Taylor liked to call me Tomas, still does). Tomas, go on out there and do your job, you heard Chuck." Taylor has this kind of precocious smile and little chuckle as he gave me those marching orders.

KEITH RICHARDS: "You heard the director and Chuck, Tom. Now go on out there and do your thing, baby."

TA: So, I go on out there and have an exchange with the perturbed lady. She showed me the scrapes on the left side of her car from the bus. And she said, "I know he's in there, I know that's Chuck Berry in there, and I want to see him right now. And he knows that I know it's him in there because this isn't the first time this has happened." I kind of talked her down and told her that we were doing the film and that we would love to have her and her family as guests for the big night at The Fox Theatre and, of course, put in an insurance claim to fix her car. So, the lady and I agreed and made arrangements to let her and her family and a few other people come into the shows in St. Louis, and I think that resolved it.

STEPHANIE BENNETT: That's when you gave her $50.00 or something.

TA: Yes, I came back in to the Winnebago and off we went to see the Cosmo Club.

CHAPTER TWELVE
Chuck Visits Keith Richards in Jamaica

PREPRODUCTION STARTS IN JAMAICA *at Keith Richard's home*
There is a beautiful estate on the Island of Jamaica. Events
have happened there that are the height of creative work in the
rock and roll business, and then there are the moments that reach
the heights of the wild and crazy world of rock and roll. And
sometimes, the twain does meet, and those moments of extremes
can swing in unison. Well, it kind of happened that way one
weekend in Ocho Rios, Jamaica during the making of Hail! Hail!
Rock 'N' Roll. *Chuck Berry, Taylor Hackford, Helen Mirren,*
and I were invited to come create, imbibe, and bond at Keith
Richard's paradise by the sea. It was only later that I realized
taking Chuck out of his normal surroundings, lifting him out of
his usual comfort zone of controlling events, would leave him
feeling essentially trapped. He cut short the planned time there,
grabbed a jet back to the USA.

TAYLOR HACKFORD: Chuck was quite an amazing
character. Keith said at our Chicago meeting that he wanted to
get together in Jamaica with Chuck, to get Chuck away from
the humdrum life he had been leading, it would be good, to
just concentrate, not be disturbed. Keith said that "Chuck
Berry is one of the great songwriters of all time, if not the
greatest, and if we could write some songs in Jamaica that we
could use in the show that would be a spectacular thing," and
I agreed with him. I said, "if you can get original Chuck Berry

songs, this is more than just a tribute concert;" this would be an amazing creative experience. So that was the attempt in going to Jamaica, and Helen Mirren and I went down to Jamaica and we went to Keith's house.

STEPHANIE BENNETT: Chuck and I and Helen and Taylor arrive at the airport in Montego Bay, Jamaica.

STEVE JORDAN: Keith and I went down to his house in Ocho Rios, Jamaica. Chuck was going to come down and meet us there so we could start working on the music, start to put a set together, and start to feel each other out and see what we wanted to do musically. At that time I had heavy dreadlocks. I looked kind of like Peter Tosh. So we went to meet Chuck at the airport. He got off the plane with a kind of polyester jacket, and pants, and a string tie, and a brief case, and it was literally close to a hundred degrees so it was a very interesting sight, and of course we were dressed in some very island gear...it was a motley crew for sure.

SB: We drove to Keith Richard's house, which was up into the hills on this very, very winding road. Keith is there, and there are all these Rastafarians walking around, smoking these huge spliffs, and you can see Chuck is obviously really uncomfortable. I think Keith or Jane showed him his room, and he disappeared for a while.

SJ: Back at Keith's house we got this little drum kit set up in the living room, and two Fender tweet amps, a couple of guitars, and then Chuck says, "well where's the drummer" and Keith says, "this is the drummer. This is the guy you wanted." And Chuck looked at me and said, "I didn't hire no Reggae drummer," and Keith says, "this is the guy you liked." Chuck had seen and heard me play on a television show, but the camera didn't have my head in the shot, so he never really knew what I looked like. He didn't know I had dreads at the time. But once we started to play, then everything was cool.

JANE ROSE: I don't think Chuck realized at first that Steve was American. He was softer when he realized he was not a Rastafarian.

HELEN MIRREN: But I think that's fairly common with Black-African Americans or Black people in America. They're uncomfortable in Africa. It's too weird for them. And I think, likewise, Jamaica. A Jamaican black person is very different from an African American black person. Obviously the countries are completely different. The understanding is different and, you know, I don't think Chuck bought into this idea that all black people are one big brotherhood, you know, of blackness. I don't think he bought into that bro stuff

SB: Just when I think things can't get worse, Chuck comes up to me and says, "I'm not staying here." And I said, "you can't do that. Keith stayed at your place, and you know what the deal is, you've got to stay here." He repeated, "I'm not staying here." Chuck asked me, "where are you staying?"

And I said, "we're all staying in a hotel." And he said, "get me a hotel room." And I was frozen. I didn't know how I was going to tell Keith or Jane that Chuck refused to stay there.

JR: I'll never forget as long as I live when he wanted out of the house. That was very upsetting to Keith. Keith said, "we're all musicians, we're all the same," but Chuck did not agree, he was not part of that same philosophy.

TH: Chuck checked into a hotel, and you can just tell that Chuck wasn't comfortable in Jamaica. Keith lived in a house staffed by Rastafarians. The Rastafarians were very cool and very efficient. They were lovely, as most people around Keith are, but all Chuck saw was long dreadlocks and smokes of these folks, and you know Chuck Berry is not a druggie…he doesn't do drugs, nor does he drink. And I think he didn't like being there. He was intimidated.

SB: And then, I remember, at one point, he actually took a puff on a joint. Everybody was smoking, and he kind of was out of it. It was funny. He said something really weird. He talked about how he didn't understand why he was so difficult or why I do these things. Something very strange, which is why I really believe he was bipolar.

TH: I also think he was intimidated because Keith was saying, "come on, man step out. Let's write a song. Get your guitar and let's write something." I don't think he had written a song in twenty years, and I think he was intimidated by the experience. I know because we were there, and immediately Keith said, "come on let's jam," and Chuck said, "I'm not jamming with anyone. I don't play any other guitar but my own." And Keith said, "you mean you didn't bring your guitar. You knew we were going to do this," and he said "no I left my guitar at the hotel." "So, Chuck, let's go to the hotel to get the guitar, and he looked at me and said, okay. They had passed a big Jamaican joint to me and I had taken a couple of tokes of this Jamaican pot and it was just unbelievably strong, so I was stoned out of my mind, and Chuck said "come on, let's go."

SJ: The road to Ocho Rios is one of the most harrowing trips you can take anywhere on the globe and we probably almost got killed a couple of times because it's a two-lane road, very winding, winding road that people drive at breakneck speeds. It's really like a Russian roulette type of ride.

TH: I wasn't going to go. But of course I said, "fine," so Chuck and I took off. Chuck's driving his rental car, and I mean Chuck is a crazy driver, as we knew from Chicago, but we drive a little. It's the British form of driving. You drive on the left-hand side, the opposite of America. So we go down the hill and Chuck doesn't know Ocho Rios, and we go down this very tropical hill and get to the main highway. Chuck drives down the wrong side of the street. In Jamaica they're not known as very good drivers either, so I mean these Jamaicans are coming at us honking their horns, and I'm stoned out of my mind. I think we're going to die. We're going along and we're literally playing chicken, going straight at a Jamaican car. He's not going to bend and I'm going, "Chuck, Chuck, Chuck," and at the last-minute Chuck pulled over and then he looked at me and smiled, and his eyebrows went up like "I gotcha didn't I?" He was fucking with me. We go to his hotel, he got his guitar, but he also made a couple of phone calls, and he was not anxious to go back to Keith's. I said, "you know, Chuck, he's got a rehearsal planned. He wants you to be there. He's brought Steve Jordan down and he really would like to rehearse. I think we should go back." So, we got in the car and we started back, and he didn't really know I was stoned.

Since I had only just arrived at Keith's house earlier, I couldn't exactly find it; although, I thought I knew and tried to remember how to get there. We went up to Ocho Rios and got completely lost. We went up over the top of the hill into a Rastafarian village, and Chuck got up on top of the car and these Rastas came out, wondering who are these tourists that are coming into our village. The villagers looked pretty hostile. Chuck rolled the window down and started speaking a kind of pig Latin to them, you know, "we want go down" to these people who were obviously pretty smart, and were looking at him and going, "what the fuck are you saying." And I'm going, "we better get out of here." It was a very definite clash of cultures. You had an American black man, who was looking down his nose at these Rastas in this village up on top. He didn't want to be there. He didn't have a lot of respect for them. And I thought, "oh, oh, this is going to erupt." We finally found our way down and the right road to get to Keith's house. When we got there, he strummed his guitar a little bit, but he basically refused to write a song, which I think was very disappointing to Keith. But, you know, it was heavy, every moment with Chuck Berry was a crisis and, at the same time, an amazing kind of adventure.

SB: I think we had another session with Keith and it was very uncomfortable. And then we went to some place where they had Jerk chicken, which is famous in Jamaica. I don't know whether Keith was there, but we went there with Chuck, and he hated it because all of the Jamaicans were calling him brother, bro, hi bro. He didn't like that at all. And then the first or second night, I was incredibly stressed out. The phone rings, and it's Chuck, and he says, "we're having drinks in the bar, why don't you come." And I said, "Chuck, I'm exhausted, thanks, but no thanks." He then proceeded to call Jane Rose, and Jane thinking that we're all there, goes. He told Jane we were all meeting in the bar, and nobody was in the bar except Chuck. Somehow he gets her to go for a walk on the beach and tries to seduce her. She told me the next day. She said, "where were you?" And I said, "I didn't go... I guess he just tricked you into going." Jane could tell the story.

JR: Oh God, on the beach in Ocho Rios. We went for a walk, and I figured, oh, it's Chuck, and I thought it was going to be nice. And we sat on the chairs, and then he put his arm around me, and I thought I would pass out, and I said, "we're working together. I can't, because we work together." I had to come up with something really fast. And then after that he would not talk to me. He would not look at me. It was a nightmare. And I remember his house and Chuck's soda in the refrigerator, the food in his house and he wouldn't let me get a soda for Keith. Oh my God. He gave me a very hard time after that. He did not forget that or forgive.

SB: Jane had been taking a lot of pictures when we first arrived at Keith's. She took pictures of Chuck in Keith's house. Then after that he forbade Jane from taking any pictures. We had one more session up at the house, and Chuck said, "I'm leaving." He said, "I don't like it here," and he got in his car and drove to the airport and left. And I remember I've got pictures. We went down to a beach and everybody was swimming. Not Chuck. He wasn't there. He left. But it was amazing he was so uncomfortable in that country, because of course everybody was black and he didn't like that at all. And he didn't like being approached, and he didn't like Steve Jordan, which then became a whole issue about the band. He was absolutely appalled with these Rastas walking around.

HM: Yes, in Jamaica he was carrying that book on Einstein. Wasn't it Einstein?

SB: Yes.

HM: It was Einstein…it was a huge tome. It was some big heavy intellectual book that he was carrying around as a statement of who he was, I thought. I mean just why that book, why carry it around everywhere…it was always with him that I remember.

SB: He didn't embrace the black. Little Richard did, but he did not embrace his race. I think he wanted to be white, which is the one thing he couldn't do. Couldn't change the color of his skin.

JR: Well, he was not comfortable in Jamaica. I think he had such a hard time that when he made it, and when Keith was going to do this, he didn't want to be pegged as another black artist. Maybe he thought everyone was trying to place him into black history. He wanted to be part of history, but not just black history. He was so articulate, and he didn't even speak like a black man. His accent was very white and homogenized. It's not a Bro at all.

SB: No, it was quite English actually, wasn't it? Well, let's face it, he traveled by himself. He picked up a van wherever we went. He used to play with Johnnie Johnson, years and years and years ago, and he played with those guys at the club, but he didn't travel with a band. He didn't travel with anyone, except him and his Cadillac. So he wasn't used to having a band imposed on him, I guess.

JR: He liked to be in control.

FEATURING

ERIC CLAPTON

ROBERT CRAY

ETTA JAMES

JULIAN LENNON

KEITH RICHARDS

LINDA RONSTADT

TAYLOR HACKFORD'S

Chuck Berry

HAIL! HAIL! ROCK 'N' ROLL

MUSIC PRODUCED BY
KEITH RICHARDS

BRUCE SI

Tomorrow Night 8 p.m

$5.50, $5.00, $4.50

Informatio

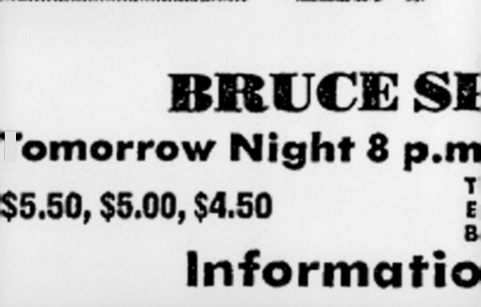

V. OF MD. PROGRAM BOARD

presents

HUCK
BERRY

and

erry Lee Lewis

NGSTEEN

Cole Field House

Montgomery Wards, Record & Tape,
cords, & Univ. of Md. Student Union
.

54-2803

Delilah Films, Stephanie Bennett, C

prese

A Delilah Films Production

Chuck

HAIL! HAIL! R

Thursday, October 8

AMC Century

10250 Santa Monica Blvd.,

Featuring Eric Clapton • Robert Cray • Etta Jar

Associate Producers Albert Spevak and Jane R

Concert Production Designed by Kim Colefax   Music Produced by Keith Richa

PG PARENTAL GUIDANCE SUGGESTED ⬥⬥⬥

SOME MATERIAL MAY NOT BE SUITABLE FOR CHILDREN ®

DOLBY ST

IN SELECTED T

Presented

MCA ®

HOME ENTERTAINMENT

ry and Taylor Hackford

A Taylor Hackford Film

'N' ROLL

:00 P.M.

es

les, California

ADMIT ONE

Lennon · Keith Richards · Linda Ronstadt

Day   Director of Photography Oliver Stapleton

ephanie Bennett and Chuck Berry   Directed by Taylor Hackford

ck Available on MCA Records and Cassettes.

A Universal Release

© 1987 UNIVERSAL CITY STUDIOS, INC.

iation with

UNIVERSAL

SONG SELECTION

# 1	SHOW # 2
ELLINE	ROLL OVER BEETHOVEN
D 'N ROUND	JOHNNIE B. GOOD
ONEY DOWN	ROCK N ROLL MUSIC
T LITTLE 16	
N EYED HANDSOME MAN	
LE QUEENIE	
O GUNN	
NA MOON	

ORMED ONLY IN SHOW # 1	PERFORMED ONLY IN SHOW # 2
IN THE U.S.A.	SCHOOL DAYS
HIS	
NEVER CAN TELL	
ARTICULAR PLACE TO GO	
IN AND ROCKIN	

NED SONGS (Version created by editing performances from both
        concerts together).

NEE HOURS	Use first part from 1st show, and last part and solo from 2nd show.
NE	1st show: Up to solo.
	2nd show: Solo to end.
ST GROWN	1st show: Create new intro and carry up to the end of first piano solo.
	2nd show: Create extra long silent pause in break after piano solo to camouflage change in tempo then carry to end of song.
MUCH MONKEY NESS	1st show: Beginning up to end of solo.
	2nd show: Start with verse "SAME THING, EVERY DAY, GETTIN' UP GOIN' TO SCHOOL..." to end dropping solo in show #2 (near end).
'N ROLL MUSIC	Possible intercut (pending investigation).

CHAPTER THIRTEEN
The Making of Hail! Hail! Rock 'N' Roll:
Nuts & Lightning Bolts

ONCE DELILAH FILMS HAD *contracted with Universal Studios to produce a feature film on Chuck Berry and we had engaged feature film director Taylor Hackford, the sculpting of the production both creatively and its approach technically had to be developed and acted on. As Taylor started to add voice and style, and create a cinematic sculpture of what my original vision for a Chuck Berry movie might evolve into, the technical journey began.* Hail! Hail! Rock 'N' Roll *was developing into a feature film which would be part concert and part documentary for theatrical release with a customary running time of approximately two hours.*

TOM ADELMAN: The challenge was enormous technically. As the creative approach was unfolding, it became clear that the photographing of the movie would have to be approached with a three-prong attack. First, there would be single camera crew (on the run) documentary style shooting in places like Chicago, St. Louis, etc. Then, there would be multi-camera coverage of rehearsals for the concert which would take place at Chuck's estate, Berry Park in Wentzville, Missouri, and include all of the guest stars who would appear as well as the backup *Hail! Hail!* band, led by musical director Keith Richards. And finally, there would be a full multi-camera shoot of what ended up being two concerts at the legendary

Fox Theatre in St. Louis to celebrate Chuck's sixtieth birthday. Everything would be shot on film. The documentary portion and the concert rehearsals would be filmed using Super 16mm film, and the concert itself would be shot on 35mm film. The rehearsals at Berry Park would include three cameras, and the concert would be covered using eight Panavision cameras and lenses. There would also be dollies on track, which would float stage left to stage right and back, from the perspective of the audience to focus on coverage of the stage as well. And at that time, the relatively unknown and unused in the United States, a French Louma crane would handle aerial coverage drifting high over the audience and the stage during both shows. The team of George T. Nierenberg and cinematographer Edward Lachman would handle the single camera shooting for the documentary portion, as well as roam the theater during the concert capturing events as they unfolded and specialized shots as per Taylor Hackford's vision. Sound wise, the entire production would be recorded by Michael Frondelli at the board as the concert recordist, utilizing David Hewitt's state of the art Remote Recording Services, Inc. company's 24-track mobile recording facility. At that time, Remote Recording Services, Inc. was one of the best state of the art companies for recording live concert presentations around the world. The movie's cinematographer was Oliver Stapleton, who hailed from the United Kingdom. During postproduction, the film was edited by Lisa Day with additional concert editing by Paul Justman. We assembled a top of the line, blue chip technical team for this movie in all departments. Jerri Lauridsen and I (she worked for Taylor Hackford), basically supervised the technical production of the movie from a St. Louis hotel room that had two telephone lines and a half-empty minibar for the duration of the show. When we first started operating out of that hotel room, the minibar was full of course. Producer Stephanie Bennett would be tied to her phone in her hotel room, locking in talent and dealing with all the other challenges that she would be faced with, mostly from Chuck himself during the entire preproduction and production period. Associate Producer and company Attorney Albert Spevak would run between his room and Stephanie's trying to connect all the legal dots in order to keep the show on track with the stars. At the time, there were no cell phones, no fax machines, no internet. Just hard phone lines and walkie-talkies to keep the channels of communication flowing. One of the first important creative choices that had to be made was choosing a director of photography and that man turned out to be British cinematographer Oliver Stapleton.

OLIVER STAPLETON: Taylor Hackford called me up in a way that British people never did, which is characteristic of Americans when they're interested in something. They just call you, and I didn't get a call from my agent, just from Taylor, who had somehow found my phone number. It was the first kind of transatlantic phone call I had, so I was very intrigued. Obviously, I knew who he was because he had already done *An Officer and a Gentleman*, so I was quite excited to get a phone call from him on many levels. One was that I knew Taylor was very good at directing music films, and I think he had probably also seen a bunch of music videos that I did. I had shot quite a lot of those at the time, prior to 1985, so I think everything added up to his phone call. I was excited on lots of different levels, working in America, working with Taylor, so yeah, it was a very intriguing call to get, really.

TA: Tell me about the first time you came to Los Angeles to meet Taylor Hackford.

OS: It was very strange. I didn't know Los Angeles at all, so the first time I had ever been to LA, Taylor picked me up from somewhere and we were traveling in his car and he said "oh well, what are you doing next." I said something like, "oh, I have to go to wherever," and then said, "well, you can just let me off and I can find my way back." For some strange reason, he did. He let me out of his car in the middle of that highway that goes to Malibu.

TA: Pacific Coast Highway?

OS: Yeah, and I didn't know you couldn't hail a cab or you couldn't get on a bus or anything. He kind of drove off, and then suddenly I was standing there thinking, "oh well, you know, there'll be a cab." I was thinking like an English cab, you just wave it down.

So for about half an hour, I was standing on the side of this deserted highway with all these cars whizzing by, and occasionally I saw a taxi and put my hand up. Of course, they didn't stop because that's not how it works, so I thought well this is really shit. So, I walked and walked and finally got to the bus stop, and of course, there was no one at the bus stop and there were no buses, and I thought well this is crap, so finally I found a guy. I said do any buses come here. And he looked at me in a strange way and went "no." So, then a really strange thing happened. A cab stopped next to me. It just came to a stop, and the guy rolled his window down and said, "are you Mr. Willis?" and right off the bat I said, "yup." And I just got in the back and I thought fuck this, you know, wherever its going, it suits me, so I went into the cab and it drives off. Anyway, I didn't talk to him, but he ends up at a hotel, which I discovered later on was the Beverly Hills Hotel and as I got out, I sort of looked at him and said listen, I'm really sorry, but

I'm not Mr. Willis and ran off. The guy was yelling out of the window after me, "Hey, you motherfucker."

TA: Had you listened to much Chuck Berry or The Rolling Stones? Did you like the music?

OS: Oh yeah, well, I worked a lot with the Rolling Stones, prior to doing the Chuck Berry film, so I knew them quite well musically, and, of course, knew that he was incredibly influential on their music. Anybody growing up in England at the time I did, there wasn't anyone who wasn't aware of Chuck Berry. His songs were so iconic, and Buddy Holly. They were all the big influences that struck us all and obviously struck our own groups at the time…The Beatles, The Stones, they were all immensely influenced by those songs.

TA: What do you recall about those initial creative discussions with you and Taylor, in terms of what you were trying to capture?

OS: Well, I went to his house. I met Helen, everybody was incredibly nice. And we basically devised the scheme for the project where we would shoot in Super 16mm, shoot the concert in 35mm using Panavision cameras and lenses. I didn't know any of the people at Panavision, because I never worked in the States, so this very strange phone call happened where I phoned up Panavision and said, "can you give me camera rental," and they kind of said, "who are you," and I said, "oh, my name's Oliver Stapleton." I could hear the person taking notes, you know, another nobody, and I get through to camera rental, and rather theatrically said, "I need eight cameras in St. Louis for Friday." I think it was Tuesday. There was a bit of a silence on the other end of the line. The person on the other end of the line said, "who's calling?" And then I said my name again, and he took me rather more seriously after that because I said, "it's a Taylor Hackford film about Chuck Berry" and suddenly Panavision put me through to somebody else. I seem to remember that we had a fantastic phone call and they were absolutely amazing. They sent all these cameras over.

TA: What were your initial chats with Taylor like creatively? What were those discussions like in terms of trying to capture stylistically this movie in terms of tone and cinematic approach?

OS: Well, one of the key decisions we made was to get the second cameraman to shoot the Super 16mm, and so we hired Edward Lachman, who I actually had never met. Ed obviously already had a bit of a reputation as an iconoclast, an outsider, an artist. I thought he would be a very interesting person to come and do the second camera, so he like anybody, jumped at the chance to see Chuck Berry and, of course, we had Keith Richards and other people turning up, so really, outside of the fact that we knew we would shoot all the documentary material on 16mm, we would not have to worry too much if it was unlit or low light or raining or any of those things. That wouldn't matter with a documentary. It would help to differentiate it.

STEPHANIE BENNETT: Throughout the making of Hail! Hail! Rock 'N' Roll, *basically only three people had Chuck's ear and attention: Taylor Hackford, the director; Keith Richards, the musical director; and myself, the producer. That was it. Anyone else was excess baggage to Chuck. So, besides having to deal with the producing side of things which was 25 percent booking artists and collaborating with Associate Producer Albert Spevak on all kinds of legal matters. The other 75 prcent was committed to handholding Chuck Berry and protecting the show. And, of course, Taylor had to approve every single technical aspect of the making of this movie. When Tom found Dave Hewitt and his*

Remote Recording Company, we had lengthy discussions about that. Tom and I reviewed all of the potential camera operators for the concert and determined who were the top choices before we submitted those names and resumes to both Taylor and Oliver Stapleton. We collaborated with the art department too. So I was pulled in a number of directions, creative, legal, booking of guests, technical, and, of course, Chuck.

TA: Oliver, during the rehearsals and during the whole production, did you have a one-on-one interaction with Chuck?

OS: No, absolutely not. As you know, Chuck was extremely difficult. Most of my interaction with Chuck consisted of sitting on an apple box just about every morning while the producers, including Taylor, would renegotiate with Chuck, usually something about the money.

As a cinematographer, it's interesting. Some artists you definitely form a relationship with at the time, which is pleasant and quite personable, and then usually when it's over you wave goodbye and you don't see each other again. Very, very, very occasionally I've stayed in touch with the odd actual musician, but it's extremely rare. But I've found on the whole that as a cinematographer you are very much behind the camera and depending on the artist, some kind of avoid you, some acknowledge you, some don't acknowledge you, but very few are rude. Most just don't notice that you're there, which is fine and that's the way it should be. It doesn't bother me with Chuck because I was very aware of the extreme difficulty for Taylor and the producers to get the film made. I was very sympathetic, and my attitude to Chuck just try not to be negative. It would be quite easy to be negative because he was very obstructive. However, I felt that wasn't my problem to deal with.

SB:*My job as producer was also to protect Taylor, Oliver, and Keith from the shenanigans that Chuck was causing, so that those three could focus on the making of the film.*

TA: I remember that every day of the documentary portion of the shoot, when Chuck would not come to the set and would insist upon more money, Taylor started shooting those diaries of himself talking to the camera, and years later, Taylor and I put together this four-disc package, using some of those diaries in a documentary in the package that he called *The Reluctant Movie Star.*

OS: I do remember that.

TA: I recall an image of you when we went to the Cosmo Club, and, if you recall, which was the first place Chuck played in St. Louis and there had been a flood or a storm the night before. The entire club was flooded, and I remember you standing in water with your hands on your hips scouting the location.

OS: I remember looking at the location and thinking, "this is a nightmare." It definitely looked like a total nightmare, but the art department, they did an amazing job restoring the club into something we could shoot. I think it was very successful. It looked great.

TA: Do you remember at the concert the whole thing with the pink Cadillac coming out on stage for the grand finale?

OS: Yeah, I definitely remember that.

TA: What was your reaction, Oliver, when you heard that Chuck passed away a few months ago?

OS: You know, I guess as these icons from that era disappear, it's interesting, isn't it? These heroes that are very much a part of your musical life, well, he wasn't huge in my life before I met him, but having made the movie and met the man, I'm afraid the polish wore very thin during the time I spent with him. So when he died, it wasn't a case of like "thank God for that," but it was a case of, "oh well, there is a genuine icon, which is now not with us anymore." It was really interesting reading the many obituaries that came out about him, because they were true. He was along, with Elvis, you know, he is rock and roll.

TA: So, are you proud of the movie, even all these years later?

OS: When the DVD box set came out about five years ago and I stuck it on the projector at home, looked at it, and I thought, "hey that's a really good movie." Yeah, I really like it, and it's a film that a lot of people know. It's, well, you know how movies are, they sometimes disappear forever, even if they're good, they sometimes vanish, but *Hail! Hail! Rock 'N' Roll*, I mean it's just a classic isn't it. It's an iconic movie. I think it catches the spirit of what was going on really well.

TA: Did you spend a lot of time talking about the movie or working with Stephanie Bennett, the producer?

OS: Stephanie was incredibly supportive and of course dealing with all that Chuck Berry stuff. I just remember thinking, "how can anyone do that job…that's terrifying." Stephanie, for me, was someone who was dealing with all the shit that was going on. Very difficult.

SB: Certainly the cinematic and production design approach to Hail! Hail! Rock 'N' Roll *was a complex and challenging endeavor, as you heard from the cinematographer, Oliver Stapleton. But then came the audio recording of the music. This was what it was all about in the end. Once we had Keith Richards signed on as musical director, he brought in veteran recording engineer Michael Frondelli to handle the actual recording all*

of the music from the rehearsals at Berry Park, as well as both
concerts at The Fox Theatre in St. Louis.

TA: Michael, how did you first become involved in the Chuck
Berry movie?

MICHAEL FRONDELLI: I had been working with Keith
Richards. We worked together on a sound track for the movie
Jumpin' Jack Flash. Keith came to me and said, "Michael, you
know I have this movie and it's got Chuck Berry. Would you
be interested in doing it?" So I think it's a rare occasion that
anybody would say no to Keith Richards. I immediately said
yes, and I said I would be more than happy for the opportunity
and that's what happened. We were working out of Electric
Lady Studios, and I remember getting a plane ticket to go
down to Wentzville to scout Chuck Berry's studio at the
request of Taylor Hackford, because Taylor wanted to know
whether or not we could record the movie audio in Chuck's
studio. I distinctly remember getting down there and meeting
Chuck, and well, there he was, Chuck Berry. And I go, "wow,
this is an incredible sight," you know he was just lounging
around, he was checking me out. I said, "I've been a fan of
your music forever, but I didn't get introduced to you directly
through your music. I was introduced to you by Johnny
Rivers." Johnny Rivers had the big hit "Memphis," and Chuck
seemed to calm down a bit. Then Taylor arrived and we went
into Chuck's studio. The roof was leaking and he had all these
vintage analog machines and guitar cases opened up with
mold on all these beautiful Gibsons. And I looked around the
room. So, Taylor looked at me and said, "so what do you think.
You want to record on this?" I said, "well, you know, there's a
video camera over there too. Would you shoot your film on
that camera?" And that started off my relationship with Taylor.

The rest is a whirlwind of traveling between New York and the planning for St. Louis.

TA: What can you tell me about Chuck and Johnnie Johnson and Keith?

MF: Keith started to sort of dissect the relationship between Johnnie and Chuck.

STEPHANIE BENNETT: Chuck was in Johnnie's original trio, The Johnnie Johnson Trio.

MF: Right, playing saxophone.

SB: Oh, he played saxophone. Did he play piano?

MF: No, Chuck played sax, that was my understanding, that Chuck played sax in the Johnnie Johnson Trio. He wasn't playing guitar. So, I thought it was kind of odd myself when I heard it at the time.

SB: But Johnnie was there at the very beginning with him at the Cosmo Club.

MF: At the Cosmo Club, yeah, that was the beginning of their relationship.

SB: And it was Keith who already knew Johnnie had a big part in Chuck's songwriting, because he insisted that Johnnie be part of the band. We had to track Johnnie down, who was driving a school bus at the time.

MF: I do remember that. He also brought Jasper Thomas in, because Jasper Thomas was the drummer. I recall meeting him at Berry Park at the rehearsal. Jasper played drums on "Sweet Little Sixteen." So I think what Keith wanted to do at the time was reconstruct this Willie Dixon–type band that played on the original records.

TA: So Jasper was brought in by Chuck or Keith?

MF: Keith.

TA: So what was the connection between Steve Jordan and Jasper then.

MF: There was none. There was no connection because the connection between Steven Jordan was with Keith in New York. They had met in New York and that was the beginning of his relationship with Keith. I knew Steve Jordan for many years, from the time he was seventeen or eighteen years old. I remember when he was a young, snot-nosed kid who was hanging around Mikell's, which was a club at Ninety-Seventh Street and Columbus Avenue. This band called the Gordon Edwards Encyclopedia of Soul would be up there with Cornell Dupree and Richard T., and the drummer would be Steve Gadd, or sometimes it was Christopher Parker. But then this little kid came in and he'd be laughing at the old men, and come on, man, you're holding me up, you know, and he'd be playing drums, and he was totally into this roots R&B thing. So Steve and Keith based their relationship on a love for vintage music. Steve was a good student and was smart enough to know that Keith was also a musical historian. And then I met Steve, because I was at Electric Lady Studios, and Steve came in on some dates. And I remember the first day I ever worked with him on his show, he was an hour late, because his mom made him clean up his room. The bass player, Joey Spampinato, was picked because he was in NRBQ, and Keith liked the style in which he played, because Joey's roots were based on Willie Dixon, and Keith wanted to assemble this kind of new band. Willie was dead, and he needed somebody who could really make that feel work. And they were really trying to get back to this old swing-style of Louie Jordon meets T. Bone Walker, meets Oscar Peterson and Nat King Cole, which is Chuck's gumbo, but that's what I recall.

TA: How was the musical interaction between Johnnie Johnston and Chuck Leavell, who was on keyboards?

MF: Chuck Leavell is a very, very sweet, humble guy, and to me Chuck was the glue because when all the insanity was going on with Chuck Berry and the changes in the keys, etc., Keith needed someone who did the homework, who looked at all the original keys, who brought the records, because I remember, and I'm sure you guys remember too, that Keith was bringing in the original recordings and playing them for Chuck, and refamiliarizing Chuck with his own music. That it wasn't just one medley of "Johnny B. Goode" and showing him the nuances. This riff was based on "Johnny B. Goode" and "Roll Over Beethoven," and finding a way to show him the differences in what he did, because Chuck got really lazy after a while, and that annoyed Keith, because he had such a reverence for Chuck's music. I think that there was an interesting moment I saw in a Johnny Carson interview with Chuck when the film was just about to be released. Chuck said that, "in those days I was making records with Leonard Chess at Chess Records and they were speeding up the records." He was saying that Keith worked him hard in the film, because he wanted to play them in the keys that he originally had done them in, not the keys that they had sped the tape up for to make the record. So, I didn't know that. We always thought that "Johnny B. Goode" was in D-flat, and its an odd key, you know, and we figured it was a piano key. So I don't know if that's revisionist history that's in the piano key in D-flat, because they sped up the tape, or whether or not it was in a different key, and Chuck was trying to communicate what originally happened to Keith.

SB: During rehearsals, how many times did he get up on stage and actually rehearse with anybody other than Keith?

MF: Well, he was up there with Eric, I think. Who else came?

TA: Robert Cray.

MF: Robert Cray came in.

TA: Etta James.

MF: I remember him with Etta. I remember him with Robert. I remember him with Eric. Julian wasn't there, Linda Ronstadt wasn't there.

SB: A lot of times, I remember Chuck was sitting there, but didn't seem to get up on the stage that much with Johnny in the rehearsals. It seemed to me that was a lot of the time. Well, as Tom says, he would disappear and be out on the tractor doing something outside.

MF: Well, Chuck had a short attention span, we knew that. But I think also, for him, he had been doing this for so long, he was bored. And his attitude was that he was going to be Chuck Berry, no matter what. And whatever they were going to do, they were going to do. And there's nothing new that they're going to show him, he hasn't seen before. Keith had his issues with that, you know, he would have preferred that Chuck be more studious about it and focused. That's why he brought all these original recordings down for him to listen to, and get reoriented on the parts and how they were played, because they are subtle. I mean, I've been playing guitar since I was eight years old. When you sit down and you listen to this stuff, each song has it's own little thing to it in guitar that you really had to focus on, but that's what made it so interesting for all of us. It was all based on the same theme, but played so many different ways, and Chuck was brilliant then. He was a brilliant poet. And, he could make things up on the spot. He could figure out a way to make it rhyme and to make it work within the melody, fit it within the bar line. He was a jazz guy, you know, he had a jazz way of dealing with the music. That's what made him so intriguing to people, and inspired these two young kids, Mick and Keith. Keith said to me, "there's not a lot money in it, but this is my payback to Chuck Berry for all the money The Stones made from Chuck Berry's music." There's a thing I want to say about Keith, because you remember Bert, Keith's dad?

SB: Yeah, I do remember him coming to the show.

MF: Yeah, he used to bring him all the time, and that was when Keith had renewed the relationship, to do the right thing for his dad at the end. You know, I look back on it now and I say, "this is a kid who was estranged from his father, because of whatever reasons. And here he is trying to do the right thing." So Keith had that odd kind of side to him, who everybody thought was a wretched rock and roller that had no boundaries, but still he had this heart of a decent man, who wanted to do the right thing, not only for his dad, but for Chuck and for music, and that's what sold me on the deal. I mean, yeah, it was Keith Richards and everything, of course, you say, yes, you don't know when that stuff comes up again. But then, do it for the right reasons. He had a great motive for what he was doing.

TA: I once asked him why he wears that skull ring. And he said, "to remind me that we're all the same...we're all the same under the flesh and the skin." And another thing he said was that he tried to live outside of his fame.

MF: That was true all of the way, and he was completely humble that way. That's why he's able to meet someone on the street, who would be a street player, and if he liked his music, he would go talk to him. You know, homeless people. When we were doing the soundtrack mix in New York City, I used to walk with Keith every morning. We would walk him from Electric Lady down to Tower Records near the triplex he lived in. You know, people came up to him all the time. He knew how to handle it. He knew how to handle people.

TA: Tell us your memories of the concert.

MF: First, I want to talk a little bit about Etta James during the rehearsals. I had met Etta when I was at Capitol. I remember Keith grabbing me and saying, "Michael, I don't know what song we want to do with Etta. Find out what she wants to do." I said, "Etta, Keith asked me to find out what you wanted to sing?" She said, "well the only song I know is 'Rock and Roll Music.'" And I said, "that's the one we'll do." Now to the concert, I remember walking in and seeing this setup that Taylor had at The Fox Theatre on the side of the stage with all these monitors, looking at all these cameras and then another camera filming behind the scenes. And I said, "oh my God, it was going to be a long night."

TA: Do you remember being in the truck and noticing there's something wrong with Chuck's voice?

MF: Oh yeah, we knew early on that his voice was just gone. He was just completely destroyed, wretched. He says this in the Johnny Carson interview too, by the way.

SB: Taylor wanted to film two shows, I don't know how much of the two of them mixed together, but the problem was that Chuck could barely sing his way through one show.

MF: And then Taylor was stopping and starting the performances to reload cameras. Keith was getting really frustrated, because you don't stop songs in the middle, you've got to go all the way through. Keith would hear "cut," and he would go out of his mind. It was totally beyond my control. All I could do was record.

TA: Stephanie, was that an invited audience or did they actually pay for tickets?

SB: They paid and that's why there was nearly a riot, because it took so long because of starting and stopping, and, meanwhile, the audience was outside cued up for the second show. I don't know what time we wrapped.

MF: I remember wrapping about two in the morning. I had a 7:00 a.m. call and I was there until two in the morning recording. We just didn't stop. We started late and then we just kept going. It was crazy.

TA: Michael, so after all of these years, are you proud of your involvement with the *Hail! Hail! Rock 'N' Roll* movie?

MF: I'm very proud of it, because Taylor said something very telling to me, "you know, we're making history here. And this film's going to live long after we're gone." That rang true, and what we do as engineers is we are recording history. We're recording a moment in time that will never occur again. And we're responsible for it's outcome. And the significance, because we don't have a film like this of Little Richard. We don't have a film like this of Fats Domino. We don't have a film like this for a lot of people. You know, at rehearsal, when I met Eric Clapton, I said, "I've always been listening to your records at half speed, which is all that was available to us in music to learn the guitar licks." And he says, "that's funny, that's how

I've been listening to it too." Eric said, "don't listen to me, listen to who I listen to and learn from the source." And that's the whole point, if you want to learn, you got to learn from the source. *Hail! Hail! Rock 'N' Roll* has that kind of significance because there is no preservation in the arts for music that way.

It's interesting, in all the publicity when he died that in all of the obituaries they mentioned *Hail! Hail! Rock 'N' Roll* because Chuck never did anything else. I mean Chuck was on *Bandstand*, but Chuck never did any interviews, you know. He never did anything after that, and I don't know that he did anything before. You didn't have a lot of wiggle room to negotiate with a guy like him. Basically, it was sort of like you were *National Geographic* catching the animal in the wild, so to speak. You know, working in his habitat. You went and shot his habitat. You shot the roots of St. Louis, and the significance of St. Louis, and what it meant in the Chitlin Circuit, and what happened in R&B. And how those regions between Chicago and St. Louis and Memphis and Nashville all somehow converged and made this rock and roll. Because, that was the whole point, that it was Chicago blues with the Chitlin Circuit in St. Louis. These were pivotal places for Ike and Tina Turner, and for a lot of artists like that. Again, we didn't see Ike and Tina Turner in a film like this telling their story. We saw *What's Love Got To Do With It*, right? You see films that are dramatizations, that are bio-pics, but you don't see the artist himself or herself shot this way.

SB: Well, we modeled it, if you remember after *The Last Waltz*, which was a combination of a concert and a documentary. That's why I initially went to Robbie Robertson and met with him. He was the first person I met with. He's the one who introduced me to Keith Richards.

TA: Yeah, that was the first meeting we went to.

SB: But I would say that with *The Last Waltz* there wasn't really any documentary. That was purely a concert film.

TA: Except there were a couple of cut-in scenes of them interviewing the band. Remember in that hotel? They're playing pool and stuff. But it wasn't as detailed as *Hail! Hail! Rock 'N' Roll*.

MF: But I think this is a lot different and I'll tell you why, because as I recall, *The Last Waltz* you're dealing with an iconic film maker like Scorcese, who puts his signature on everything. He was also a huge fan of *The Band*, which I think in a way was not a good thing. I mean it was a great film, but it didn't tell a story like *Hail! Hail!* did. I'll tell you why. What I didn't know about Taylor Hackford before I met him was the fact that he worked in news, that he worked in television news, which is a different perspective when you're doing a documentary like this.

He worked in TV news in California, which makes a difference as a journalist, looking at it from a journalistic perspective. This film was done in real time. That's the difference, you caught him at the beginning of the sunset, so to speak, of Chuck Berry's life in his last and basically the third act, and it was an interesting perspective that you guys shot that way, because I've not seen anything like this in that way where you get to be yourself in your own film and you capture scenes that are nice and neat that way, wrapped around a concert.

TA: And a piece of history for sure.

MF: Exactly, its historical in that sense. And I think that it doesn't get the credit for that as a film piece.

CHAPTER FOURTEEN
The Cosmo Club
Production Starts: Where's Chuck

STEPHANIE BENNETT: *We were filming a fifties period reenactment of a gig Chuck had done at The Cosmopolitan Club in East St. Louis, Illinois, across the river from St. Louis, Missouri. The club, in what was considered one of the most dangerous areas of East St. Louis, was the first place Chuck had performed regular gigs, having taken over from Johnnie Johnson and his group in the fifties. It was run down and, because of the rain from the day before, was flooded. The film's art department pulled off a miracle and fixed it up. Chucks call time to be at the location was 8:00 a.m.*

TOM ADELMAN: Everything was set to go and all the contracts had been signed, and all the guests had been booked, and all the crews flown into St. Louis, and all the cameras were loaded, but Chuck Berry didn't show up. Here we all were on the first day of shooting on the set. Taylor Hackford was excited and he's got an A-level crew from all parts of the country, the best guys from the West and East Coast on his team. And Chuck Berry is a no show?

TAYLOR HACKFORD: After the horrible experience at Algoa state prison where we went out and had all this wonderful stuff, and then Chuck took the tape and I couldn't use it, we weren't able to shoot our first day, because the prison wouldn't let us come back. And so, I had other things set up, and the new first day of shooting would be at the

Cosmo club, in East St. Louis, Illinois. Now East St. Louis is a very tough black enclave and at the time there was no police force. The National Guard patrolled the streets. We got over to the Cosmo Club at six in the morning, and I had said to Chuck the night before that I was going to pick him up the next morning. Nope. "Nobody drives Chuck Berry, but Chuck Berry, right." Okay. He would get there himself. I said, "do you need a reminder." "No, I'll be there. What time do you want me there?" I said, "I want you there at seven a.m. because we're going to be there at six a.m." So the next day comes and we are all set up. Seven a.m. rolls around, and no Chuck Berry. And I wait and I wait and I wait, and I'm worried. About fifteen minutes go by, half hour goes by, well you know, maybe something happened. I call out to Wentzville and I talk to Fran, his assistant. She says, "oh no, Chuck left. He left here at quarter of six." That's weird. Maybe something happened on the highway. Anyway, 7:30 comes, 7:45 goes by. Now it's getting late and I've got a crew there. I'm very concerned. Well, I'm standing there on this street, this kind of war zone of East St. Louis, Illinois, and on the corner a pay phone starts to ring. Now I listen to this pay phone, and I'm thinking, "well some pimp is trying to make connection with his whore or there's a dope deal going down." Not saying anything against East St. Louis, but it's a tough neighborhood, right. I mean it's a pay phone, right, on the corner. Somebody says, "leave it alone." So it rings and rings and rings. Finally one of the crew members go over and picks it up just because it had been ringing so long. And he says, "it's for you." Someone calling me on a pay phone. I go over to the pay phone and I said, "Hello." He says, "Taylor." I said, "Chuck, where are you? Is everything all right? Did you get into an accident?" "No, no, everything's fine." "So, where are you Chuck?" He says, "Taylor I just wanted to make this call to tell you everything is cool between you and me." I said, "well, that's great, Chuck, what does that mean? When are you going to get here?" He says, "let me talk to the producer." And I said, "do you want to talk about it, Chuck?" "No, let me talk to the producer." So I hand the phone to Stephanie Bennett. Again it's a quarter to eight on a Saturday morning or a Sunday morning in East St. Louis, Illinois, and I hear her saying, "but, Chuck, Chuck, Chuck, the banks aren't open. Chuck, where am I going…" then she hangs up. She turns to say he won't come unless he gets a bag full of money. And she had to now leave and go out to negotiate with him.

SB: *All the crew, everything was in place, and we get this call (no cell phones in those days) but somehow he had the number of the phone box. Chuck had been with us the day before when we were scouting so I assume he took the number down then or maybe he knew it from the old days, anyway, it was a cute way to get in touch with me. When I picked up the phone I said the same as Taylor, "where are you?" He said, "you need to get your lawyer and come out to Berry Park." I said, "you are holding up the filming," but my pleas where to no avail. I went out to Berry Park and Chuck says shooting at the Cosmo is not in the deal we agreed to and I want more money. He also alludes to my rejection of him saying, "I told you it would cost you." I called Albert Spevak who was as usual doing paperwork at a hotel in St. Louis and said, "you should come out to Berry Park."*

ALBERT SPEVAK: You would call me almost every morning and say, "you've got to get out here. We have to renegotiate something with Chuck." This would happen daily until Universal told us to have Chuck write his demands in the hope we could claim duress later.

TH: Well, anyway, we're just waiting. I've talked to Stephanie and I've talked with Albert and they said, "just wait," so that's what we're doing. It's now two o'clock and we're at lunch. And so far we've gotten intermittent phone calls from the negotiation site that Chuck is still working on his deal and meanwhile the crew is all set up now, completely lit. We shoot pick-up shots every place we can, and wait.

STEPHANIE BENNETT: You know, the show had to go on, so basically we had to agree to his demands.

TH: The film was being held hostage by its star.

SB: Yes, it was being held hostage by the star.

TH: Finally after lunch, in the middle of the afternoon, he shows up. I have a little bit where he's driving up in a car, and I'm kind of trying to clandestinely shoot him. And I don't know if he's going to stay or not. And immediately he knows that the camera is going. You know Chuck is very slick. And then we set things up and he was sweet as pie. Chuck was always great with me. Once he worked out his deal, he understood that the director was his person, and he was incredibly charming to the camera.

SB: So we worked it out with Chuck, and finally Chuck shows up having agreed to another fee of around $25,000. That night the Cosmo Club shoot was packed, and because it was where he played in the fifties when no white people were allowed, Chuck had to make a statement as Jane Ayer, the publicist from Universal remembers.

JANE AYER: Well, we're there and Chuck says to me, "I want you to sit up in the front row of the Cosmopolitan," and I felt kind of awkward to be there, because I'm the only white person in the whole club and I'm a blonde to boot.

SB And it was set in the fifties, so there wouldn't have been any white people there. But Chuck wanted to make some kind of a statement.

JA: He wanted me to have a good seat where everybody could see a white girl in the front row, but later, Albert and Tom showed me the footage and then they showed me how they edited me out of that footage. But for me, it was great, because I sat up there, and I got to watch him play.

SB: It was a typical thing Chuck would do, because in the days when he did the Cosmopolitan, white women were not allowed in. He kept making statements like that all the time.

TH: That stuff in the film where he's in the Cosmo Club and talks about being there and that night we invited an audience. The Cosmo Club, when we went there, it had been burned out. There were holes in the roof and I mean Stephanie said, "we can't shoot here." I said, "we are going to shoot here." It's not in that bad a shape, and so we made the place look as good as possible. I think we did make it look pretty damned good. And we shot the concert there. I wanted to get that sense of what it was like on stage at the Cosmo in a black community. It was an all black audience when Chuck Berry was first starting. And, sure enough, Chuck Berry knows what he's doing. He goes up on stage. He had some local musicians that he knew and liked. And they played. And it was a way for me to start the movie. I started with "Maybelline," because he came out of the Cosmo Club, went to Chicago and recorded "Maybelline." We did get our first day's shoot, and lo and behold it was pretty damned good. When he finally came almost seven, eight hours after we were there, it was a late night, but once I went in and got it, he was fantastic. So our first day at the Cosmo Club was very, very cool. So now, every day after that turned out to be a replication of that same thing.

SB: I would pick Chuck up in the morning and say, "what's the problem." He would say, "the problem is we don't have an agreement for today's shoot," and I would say, "it is my understanding we did have an agreement." He said, "no that was an agreement for yesterday's shoot." And he said, "again, you better get your attorney out here," and I said, "no. What do you want, just write it up." He said, "well I wouldn't do that if I was you. I would really advise you to have your attorney here." I said, "just write it up and I'll sign it." The lawyers from Universal said rather than negotiate, just have Chuck write up a new agreement each time I went there. And he sat at a little portable typewriter himself and typed and kept rewriting the contract every day.

TH: We were supposed to go out to Chuck Berry's old neighborhood and talk with him about his early life, his family. We were going to go to his sister's house, where his father, who is about ninety-three years old lives. He's talked a lot about his father and we wanted to get his father on film. I think he also wanted to get his father in the film. But this morning I got a phone call from Chuck saying he was not going to be able to come today. He was ill and that may very well be so, but this has now happened on a fair degree of regularity and he hasn't been ill. We are hoping to be able to get things in the film that we think are important to him, and it's getting increasingly frustrating that we've come all this way and money is being spent. At the same time, it seems as though things that he's agreed to, things that we talked about doing with him, he's changed his mind. Second of all, he asked the producer and the associate producer to go out and negotiate again.

Taylor couldn't believe that Chuck pulled the same thing everyday and wanted to know how much he was getting.

SB: I think it started at something like $150,000 and ended up at something like $800,000.

TH: He knew he had us by the short and curlys. He knew it, and in this instance he was bound and determined to squeeze every amount of cash he could, and that's what he did over the course of this. Well, after the Cosmo Club shoot, we then went out to Berry Park and we were shooting rehearsals, and it was very cool. And Robert Cray was one of the first people, and I've got a great thing where he's doing "Come On." Eric Clapton shows up, Julian Lennon shows up,

Linda Ronstadt is coming to town. Everything is working okay, and then I'm getting ready to shoot the next day. I've got it all planned out. We're going to go and we're going to meet his father. And I really wanted to get his family in this movie. I thought that was very important. I say, "Chuck, we're going to be doing the following the next day. We're going to be here, here," and he says, "oh, I can't shoot tomorrow." I said, "you can't shoot tomorrow, what do you mean? I've got five days for this entire schedule. Chuck, we've got these things set up." He says, "I can't shoot. I'm going to Columbus, Ohio, I'm playing a gig there." I mean, no one had heard this.

CHAPTER FIFTEEN
An Unscheduled Trip to Ohio

ALTHOUGH CHUCK KNEW THE *filming dates, he took a gig to perform in Columbus, Ohio. There was nothing we could do about it. He just was going to go and do his gig because he committed to it. I guess it shows you that in a way he didn't think our film was any more important than this gig at some state fair.*

TAYLOR HACKFORD: I said, "well, cancel it." He says, "hey man, I ain't cancelling it. They paid me $25,000.00. I ain't cancelling it." And at this moment I came to the realization, this kind of provocation had been happening every day. I was getting a little pissed. I kind of walked away, thinking, "what the hell am I going to do. I'm going to lose an entire day shoot." And then I said to myself, "do you know what, he's not going to get me on this." I went back and said, "Chuck, I'm coming. We're going to fly with you to this gig." He went, "hey, you want to buy your own ticket, that's fine with me. I ain't buying it." And it turned out to be a fantastic element of this movie and I'll tell you why. We went out to the airport, we saw him park his Cadillac. He parked it in the short-term car park. I said, "why, don't you want to be here longer? Are you going to stay overnight?" "No, I'm not staying overnight. I'm coming back tonight." I thought that was pretty interesting. He gets on the plane. He's flying first class. When you see him walking through the airport in St. Louis there are two things that hit me today, you know thirty years later looking at this. TWA doesn't exist any more. That was the whole hub for TWA, a very important airline in the United States. And they knew Chuck Berry. I think he said he had a million miles logged with TWA, travelling so often every week. In watching him walk through that airport, you know, kind of proud and tall and he's walking very cocky. And he's wearing that polyester outfit from the seventies. This was in the late eighties and still to this day, Chuck Berry wears kind of seventies' garb. He liked it when he got it in the late sixties and seventies and he's still wearing it. He's carrying his briefcase; he checks his guitar. We went with Chuck to Columbus, Ohio, and it was like watching a machine. He had done this a million times. He meets the band, changes into yet another seventies' outfit, grabs his guitar, and goes on stage and starts playing. The band has to catch up, but the audience loves it, and later I spoke with Bruce Springsteen, who was the top rock star in America, and it turns out that Bruce and his band had gone through this same drill. They had backed up Chuck early in their career, and I ended up using Bruce to narrate our trip to Columbus, and the thing that was fantastic is that nothing had changed in ten years. Probably nothing has changed in thirty years. Chuck has the same drill.

BRUCE SPRINGSTEEN: I met Chuck Berry once when my manager said, "gee, you know you're going to open the bill for Jerry Lee Lewis and Chuck Berry." And we thought this was forget it, I was twenty-three or twenty-four and these guys were our heroes, and we were real excited, and he said he gotta get a band to back up Chuck Berry. And we said, "no, no don't get one of the local bands." I was telling him we'll back him up. I think my first album might have just come around that time. So, we went down to Maryland, we drove in from some overnight gig. We came out and played for about a half hour, which is what generally the time we were allotted in those days if you were an opening act. It went over pretty good. Then Jerry Lee came out, and he did his set and standing on the piano and Chuck Berry, right…not there, so it's about…I forget what time he was supposed to go on. It was getting very close to the time he was supposed to go on. No sign of him. The promoter's getting really nervous. He comes up to me and says, "look go on back out there, because Chuck Berry's not here. I don't think he's coming." So, I'm not going to go out there. They're waiting for Chuck Berry….we're not going to go on again and about five minutes before the show was timed to start, the back door opens, he comes in, he's by himself and he's got a guitar case and that was it. I guess he pulled up in his own car. He didn't have anybody with him and he kind of walked behind me and went straight to the office of the promoter. I think the rumor was he would get eleven grand and at the end of the night he'd give a grand back if the band was okay and the equipment worked. I don't know if that is true, but that's what we heard. So straight into the office and then he comes out of the office and he comes to the band, and I said, "great, we're going to go on," and I said, "what songs are we going to do." And he says, "well, we're going to do some Chuck Berry songs…" that's all he says, so we go, "okay." We get out on stage, the crowd's going insane. I can see him and he walks on, opens up the guitar case, tunes his guitar. The lights are up and the place is going nuts, and we're going like, "what are we going to start with Chuck," and he's not paying attention to us and then all I see is (hammers beat) and that's it and the band is like, "yeah we're in a state of total panic;" we're trying to figure out what song are we playing, what key is it in and Chuck plays in a lot of strange keys: B-Flat, E-Flat, and our bass player, he's kind of the historian of the band, so everybody runs to him and he has the right key, and so we pick up the key and we're doing pretty good I think. I forget what song it was, but we're playing away and the crowd's going nuts and Chuck runs back and says, "play for that money, boys." We were told we weren't getting any money. Anyway the night ended and a big brawl in front of the stage and the lights came up and I think his amp blew up. I guess we were doing "Johnny B. Goode," and we're just playing that rhythm. And he just kind of walked offstage and right on the side of the stage, he packed his guitar right in front of the entire auditorium. They're going crazy. He waved. That was it. He walked out. Walked back to his car and he was gone. I don't know if he got these memories. We were probably just one of those bands he was using on the road at the time. It was just like, you know, when I'm sixty-five, seventy, I got my grandkids, "Chuck Berry, yeah, I met Chuck Berry. As a matter of fact I backed Chuck Berry up one night." "You did?" "Yeah," that's the story I'm always going to tell. Probably like most musicians of my generation, I first really heard Chuck Berry through The Rolling Stones. I think I learned my first Chuck Berry lead through Keith Richards, probably. The first Rolling Stones record I think they had "Carol" and a few other Chuck Berry songs on. And then I kind of went back and got his records, and I guess the funny thing was I think his influence on my own writing came out more later on when I wanted to write the way I thought that people talked, because that's how I felt, that's how he writes. If you listen to one of his songs, it sounds like somebody's coming in, sitting down in a chair, and telling a story about their aunt or your brother or, ah, describing some girl, descriptiveness, and his eye for detail, like "Nadine." I've never seen a coffee-colored Cadillac, but I know exactly what one looks like.

STEVE JORDAN: He started to take some gigs in the middle of rehearsal, and one thing in particular was the Ohio State Fair I believe, and he took the job really pretty close to game time, you know. Here we are, we know that this show is going to be pretty exhausting. It's going to take a lot. And he took a show, I guess, two or three days before our Fox show in St. Louis. And, of course, he did the show, he made his money, but he lost his voice. So he had no voice for the show, which kind of made everybody panic.

TAYLOR HACKFORD: He was in a way screwing over his own movie in order to make an extra twenty-five grand. I happened to get some good stuff for the film. But, unfortunately, what happened that night. You know Chuck feels he's invincible. He was sixty years old. He is pretty tough and very sinuated. We wish we all are in that great a shape at sixty, but that night out in the cold night air of Columbus, Ohio, screaming at the crowd, he got the flu, he got a cold. I happened to get some good stuff for the film.

CHAPTER SIXTEEN

The Chuck Berry Rehearsals: Keith and Chuck Go Head-to-Head

ON THE BERRY ESTATE, there was a large, well, let's call it a clubhouse he once used as a studio in years gone by. It had a small stage and, off to the side, a long bar. It was fairly spacious. The red carpets, the mosaic, and collage of colors in the couches and chairs, representing all eras of furniture design. It had an interior look and condition that alluded to grander days gone by. It was not the usual rehearsal space that our stars of the show were used to, but it being in Chuck's house was unique and considering his desire for privacy, it was surprising he allowed us to use it. So they gathered and the roadies set up the amplifiers, and the microphones, and the keyboards, and we had Chuck's dusty old piano tuned for Johnnie Johnson. Taylor Hackford had the three Super 16mm cameras positioned. Recording engineer Mike Frondelli had the 24-track remote audio recording truck parked outside and wired up to record these rehearsals from inside the clubhouse.

JANE AYER: I thought it was totally Chuck Berry. It seemed really normal to me in a way. And the recording studio was just pretty funky, but was cool. Where we sat down and had our lunch, it was sort of like a little fifties deli, and all the posters on the wall. I loved those sixties posters, which were the real posters, you know from San Francisco. I looked at all of them. They were the real thing. They were all Chuck and Jefferson Airplane and all the other bands.

How would Eric Clapton, Etta James, Keith Richards, Robert Cray and the others react? Unpainted and in some places rotting building exteriors, a large guitar shaped swimming pool with leaves and other signs of nature's signature laying on the bottom, overgrown grass uncut in areas, maybe for years, and other signs of abandonment left only memories of a glorious past. This was like entering a ghost town. But they came and the stage was set, literally for some of the most historical and strange rehearsals any of these famous musicians had probably ever taken part in.

TOM ADELMAN: If you recall that scene from Peter Bogdanovich's classic movie *The Last Picture Show,* where you see tumbleweeds and dust blowing down an abandoned rural street like you were in the middle of the Dust Bowl, well, that's what Berry Park kind of reminded me of when I first entered its gates, but the artists showed up, and the crew showed up and the producer and the director showed up. But you know who didn't show up? That's right, you guessed it, Chuck Berry. And because Chuck Berry was also the caretaker of this property known as Berry Park, well, when grass had to be cut, or land had to be flattened, or the tractor had to be switched on, he was gone. And it did not matter that a "who's who" of rock and roll royalty and legends were waiting on that little stage to work with and honor him, it just didn't matter to Chuck. So, they waited patiently, and they did what musicians in waiting do, they jammed, and some of our most memorable moments of the rehearsal experience was sitting on a couch directly in front of that little stage and watching in awe, just a few feet in front of us, some of our personal musical heroes finding the pocket and letting it all blow. Eventually, he showed up with his legendary Gibson ES 335 stereo guitar slung around his shoulder as if he were heading to the OK Corral to stand his ground. He sat and he watched the band, led by Keith Richards with Steve Jordan on drums, Joey Spampinato on bass, Bobby Keyes on tenor saxophone, Chuck Leavell on keyboards, and, of course, Johnnie Johnson on piano. Keith led them through Chuck's repertoire right in front of the father of rock and roll, and Chuck played occasionally, sometimes sitting on his armchair in front of the stage, sometimes sitting in his chair on the stage, and he laughed, and he argued, but he would not be led by any band leader, including Keith Richards. The cameras rolled, the sound was recorded, and these rehearsals were underway. This historical musical summit started to take shape and sculpt itself into a tight and swinging band. And all of it was captured on camera.

JANE ROSE: Keith would be at rehearsal at 11:00 a.m. and say, "okay, where is Chuck?" And he'd be at his motel or with some woman, and Keith is saying, "where is Chuck. It's eleven o'clock and we're starting rehearsals." I remember when Keith yelled over some Kentucky Fried Chicken, which was my newfound discovery when I was down there, and Johnnie got off the piano to come and eat, and Keith yelled, "what the hell are you doing bringing food in here." Johnnie said, "we're having a food break, Keith, I'm sorry." He took the job seriously, and it was the first time I had seen him do anything like this. He wanted it to be perfect. He wanted to do the best job he could do for Chuck because he owed him so much and he had so much regard for him. He just wanted to do a great job, but he loved it. He loved it.

TA: Julian Lennon came to the rehearsals. I remember we were short of vehicles, and I had to fetch him in a pickup truck at the airport that we borrowed from someone.

We didn't use one of Chuck's Cadillac's as he would have charged us by the mile.

JA: I remember that I was at Chuck's home, at Berry Park, in the recording studio, and I had worked with Julian Lennon before, and then Julian was happy to see me. He introduced me to Eric Clapton, and we all sat in that little booth at Chuck's house, which is amazing. It was like a little fifties deli, so it was really exciting to see them and to watch the behind-the-scenes rehearsals. It was just the most exciting thing I had ever done. And I had worked with The Rolling Stones. I had worked with Ringo. I worked a lot with Led Zeppelin. I worked with big, big acts, Elton John. But this was different. This was, like, really exciting.

As you well know, dealing with Chuck was a nonstop cyclone of drama, but when those guys started to play, it brought it all into focus for me, and I'm sure for you and others. I mean, it was really historic watching Keith Richards and the band try to force Chuck into taking these rehearsals seriously. And he was so disrespectful to some of these artists. He wouldn't let Jane get a soft drink for Keith from the fridge, can you imagine?

STEPHANIE BENNETT: Choosing the right mixture of musicians for this once in a lifetime lineup of a Chuck Berry band was a lot more challenging than one might imagine. The nucleus of the rhythm section had to be absolutely pitch-perfect in order to recreate the real sound that Chuck had laid down with Johnnie Johnson at that studio in Chicago. And there were only a few musicians who understood the nuts and bolts of what made-up Chuck's recordings in order to reproduce authentically the sound that came off that needle when the vinyl rolled. Keith, with the help of Steve Jordan, had assembled a band made-up of the best musicians on the planet who were the right lineup to capture that sound, that authentic Chuck Berry sound, which had not been attempted since the early days of Chuck recording in Chicago at Chess records when, the songs were played on an upright bass. Joey Spampinato, one of the founding members of the band NRBQ was brought in as the bass player, and according to Steve Jordan, about the only guy who could do the job.

JOEY SPAMPINATO: People instinctively played, what needed to be played. Everybody trusted everybody in doing what they do. Nobody telling anybody how to play or anything like that, just a natural experience, and everybody just had fun. We just grew and we all came together.

—

SB: As the rehearsals got underway, there were glorious moments of band mates, swinging in musical harmony, but there were also clouds of unbridled friction, usually between Chuck and Keith. One of those moments was the famous "Don't touch my amp" episode as seen in the movie Hail! Hail! Rock 'N' Roll. *Chuck never rehearsed, so this was a new experience for him.*

Setting: Berry Park Rehearsal Studio (from the film):

CHUCK
Don't touch my amp.

KEITH
He already said he didn't,

CHUCK
Well, he said, why it's being done.

KEITH
Why it's being done?, because it's not recording well. And that's the way it's going to end up on the film, right?

CHUCK

If that's the way it ends up on the film, that's the way Chuck
Berry plays it, you understand?

KEITH

I understand, I understand.

CHUCK

Well, I was talking to him about it.

KEITH

You're gonna live with it after.

CHUCK

I've been living for sixty years with it.

KEITH

I know that.

CHUCK

OK, well, then realize it.

KEITH

But is it gonna be here after we're all dead and gone.

CHUCK

Well, I ain't dying.

—

TA: Michael, this was one of the most talked about moments from our movie. The audio team was trying to give Chuck the best sound and Chuck resisted any kind of outside control over his rig. And we all thought, "well, that's Chuck again," wrapping himself up in a protective bubble of disruption and confrontation, which we had all basically grown accustomed to. But, in interviewing Steve Jordan, who was really Keith's partner and musical technical architect, we discovered that there were different perspectives on what had happened in this stunning confrontation between Keith and Chuck. It all kind of started with you, Michael Frondelli, our recording engineer. During the rehearsals, you were behind the audio recording board in the truck. Do you remember the famous incident where Chuck and Keith get into it over, who was it, the roadie, who turned the amp up and they go off on that whole thing?

MICHAEL FRONDELLI: Yes, I was the cause of that.

TA: What happened?

MF: What happened was that Chuck had this huge amplifier on stage and the guitar he plays is a Gibson 335 as a stereo guitar, so there's two outputs. So Chuck would have two channels and would split the outputs and put it on stage and stereo speakers. Chuck would have his guitars on two and the amp on ten, so when he wanted to be really loud, he would just rip the volume on his guitar, and just get it real loud. But, you know, it's just a horrible sound, and Chuck for years and years just didn't give a shit. I called Keith into the truck and I said, "you should listen to what Chuck's sound is," and I said, "check this out." And he said, "that's terrible." And I said, "yeah, I know." I said, "I don't know what to do." I said, "it sounds like it's all noise and then he just turns it all up and it just blows everybody else away." And Keith Richard says, "I'll get Alan Rogan, my guitar technician to do something about it." And I said, "okay, you know, it would be nice if we had a real Chuck Berry sound," and if you see in the film, if you recall. Keith had bought two guitars for Chuck to choose from for the show, and they were the original Gibson Blonde ES 350s. It's the ones that Eric Clapton used in the show. And Keith was suggesting that Chuck should use that, but he didn't want to do that. And, but as we mistakenly thought he really did care about his tone, he wanted it the way Chuck

Berry did it. Keith had Alan Rogen going behind the scenes without Chuck and Steve Jordan being aware, and just sort of tweaking it to get a decent guitar sound for Chuck for the rehearsal, because Keith knew we were recording rehearsals but as we discovered, perhaps Chuck was right to insist how it should be.

STEVE JORDAN: Are you kidding! Probably the most talked about moment, it was the perfect. It kind of summed up the whole institutionalized, ah, I'm not going to say institutionalized racism, but I will say the kind of narratives that goes with somebody who is genius and then, over the years, you think the person doesn't really know what they're doing because of how the learning career arc or personal life arc or whatever. I'm going to tell you exactly what happened. So what Chuck was playing through was a Fender bass, like a bandmaster. It was a big bass; it was a big amp, they were trying to control his sound from another amplifier off stage. So in other words, there was an amp on stage and a cabinet, and so they rigged it to where they could operate the amp from off-stage from another amp and just have the speaker on stage, but the amp that was on the stage was kind of bypassed, so the thinking was, and nobody talked to me about this, because if they had, I would have nixed it immediately because it was extremely condescending. So this guy convinced Keith, look, we could do this thing where he could control the sound off the stage, but nobody discussed this with me.

JS: As we were playing, somebody came around and started fiddling around with the knobs on Chuck's amp. And, at first I don't think it was noticed, I didn't even notice it too much when it first started, but then, all of a sudden, it seemed like it started to become a thing. And Chuck noticed it and didn't like it, and realized that his sound was changing, and he didn't like that. So Chuck took a stand on it and he said, "don't mess with my guitar amp." That's the way I remember it. They were trying to make it so that Keith's guitar and Chuck's guitar sounded different and clear, good sounding and different from each other.

SJ: But at any rate, there was an easier way to do it. In other words, all you have to do is just adjust the sound all on the stage. You don't have to be subversive, insult the guy who invented the friggin' thing that got you, no Chuck Berry, no Rolling Stones. You do not treat a human being like that. You're paying tribute to this guy. The next thing you know you're thinking that he's a basic asshole by going around him. Now Keith's sanctioning of this is probably because he just wanted to make sure that Chuck sounded good after we're all dead and gone and everything. There was a better way to do it, and I'm sure Keith was concentrating on getting the music right, so he didn't put a lot of thought into what it would have done to Chuck's feeling or even that Chuck was hands on about his sound. But there was another way to do it. You either discuss it with him or whatever, but you don't do it the way it was done.

TA: So actually, in reality, Chuck being angry. There was a legitimate motivation for him to be upset.

SJ: Oh absolutely, absolutely. He went to adjust his sound and it didn't change and he wanted to know why, and then he found out because he was being made an ass out of. Basically, he said, "hey, you see the sound isn't changing because that amp up there is a dummy amp and so, basically, you've been hoodwinked."

TA: I think you're right, because in the movie Chuck is screaming at the roadie, because he saw him adjusting the volume or something.

SJ: Right, so basically, what you have there is the same thing that's been happening to Chuck Berry now for thirty-five years: whether it's the Mann Act, whether its Brian Wilson ripping off rock and roll music. You name it. And now he's coproducing a film about himself, and it's still happening. So, he must have been so angry, which you captured on the film. He probably was more angry than the film captured. And I was sitting there going, what are you frigging guys doing, how did this happen? Why are you doing this? Nobody even discussed it with me. So basically, he had every right to be angry. So that's when he took it out on Keith to play the exact lick that he played on "Carol."

TA: Steve, very few people are going to try and instruct Keith Richards and give him a lesson on how to play something on the guitar. Tell us about that?

SJ: So now he's saying basically, "okay you guys want to play like the original." Okay, well, I'm going to play like that. My "Carol" lick goes like this, and here now that he's being refamiliarized with his genius, he remembers everything that he did and why he did it. So Keith had to play a version of what Chuck played on "Carol," but not exactly what Chuck played, and he wants you to play exactly what he played. And Keith couldn't do it, because basically for Keith it was some kind of a throw-away part. But it wasn't a throw-away part, nothing that Chuck Berry ever wrote or played was a throw-away part. He knew exactly what he was doing, and he could forty years later play it back for you, and it was exactly what he did in the film. He said to Keith, "no, it goes like this," and he played it again and again. And Chuck kept injecting into the rehearsal, "you gotta get it right." But, this wouldn't have happened if they hadn't try to go around him and make him look like a jerk. It wasn't their intention to make Chuck look bad. They wanted Chuck to sound good later on in the film, but it wasn't executed correctly. Consequently, it opened up Pandora's box about everything that Chuck Berry ever had to go through when he became a professional, whether it was going to a club and the club owner telling him, "Well, you're not the guy who wrote 'Maybelline.' You know, you're black. That guy's white." It brought everything back.

TAYLOR HACKFORD: When you're a documentarian, you have this stuff going on, you're just licking your chops. It's like such an amazing, its brilliant, because you get two incredibly strong personalities meeting, clashing, and you know, Chuck was like pissed at Keith. He doesn't want to be there rehearsing, and he was pissed that Keith was making him do it, so he made him pay by humiliating him. And to me, again, that was such a brilliant example of Keith Richards' strength. Instead of being a spoiled rock and roll star, and stomping out and saying "fuck you, this is embarrassing to me and they're shooting it," he stood his ground. He's a man. He knew Chuck Berry's a man. Keith Richards is a man and they dueled it out, two gunslingers, they dueled it out and, in the end, I think Keith Richards won. You know Keith sat through it and he got great material from Chuck, and the thing that's great is when they had that breakdown, and then they start playing again, and when they go back to "Carol" and Chuck finishes the song, the thing is to me one of my favorite musical moments in the whole film, because they are kicking ass. I kind of remember Steve Jordan looking back and saying, "oh God, what is happening here." And when they finally started playing, everything was such a relief and Chuck was laughing. It was just...the band was really cooking, and they finished the song and I went, "wow." There had been a moment which was destructive, and everything was decomposed at the end and a half ass performance, but instead it had this breakdown and you had this incredible personnel playing, you had this great sensitive moment, ah, humiliation, and then Keith didn't back down and then the band then starts playing and the music is fantastic...but boy it's a great song. It's real rock and roll. And that man was cooking. It kind of...you know it's like the relief that happens when the tension's been on, but they're playing their asses off. So again, it's alive, it is alive in the film. There are things that you knew were not rehearsed, couldn't have been rehearsed, that were dramatic and at the same time, musically fascinating.

JS: I'm in a hotel room with Keith and Steve, and they were having rehearsal experiences with Chuck Berry already. And, they said, at some time during these rehearsals, "Chuck is gonna give you a music lesson. He's gonna put you on the floor and show you what it is all about." And I was really nervous about it. As it turned out, at some point during the rehearsals something came up in one of the songs and I was playing a beat line on it, kind of, like, the character of the song and that bass line did a certain thing none of the other songs did. And that was the way it was played on the record, but Chuck was correcting me. But, over the years, things evolved and I guess it wasn't played like that anymore. So Chuck didn't even remember it. So I was telling him that's the way it was originally played on the record, Chuck, but I said to Chuck,

"can do it the way you want to if you want to change it now."
And that's kinda where it was left that day. And the very next
day, we were waiting for him to come in. And, he comes in,
and Chuck says, "you were right!" He wanted to know and
he went back to it and listened to it himself. It was a stunning
moment, Chuck actually admitting that I was right about the
bass part.

TA: Joey's experience was a bit different than Keith's lesson
from Chuck on "Carol."

Steve, is that the way things evolved through the rest of
the rehearsal. Like you're gonna get it the way Chuck Berry
plays it guys.

SJ: Well, it was not really who was in control of the band,
because obviously Keith was in charge of doing that formally,
you know. I mean, Chuck was very cognizant of the form of the
songs, which was very great to have him be able to have that
role. There's no warning on any of the original music okay, so
Chuck was kind of just the glue, not overplaying, but he knew
the songs. He was kind of in the role of glue, you know what
I mean, and if we got to the chorus before there was another
verse, Chuck was the one who said, "hold on." We went to the
chorus too soon or maybe there's one more verse here, so that's
the role that he took on. After I got the key members of the band
together, I took on the role of high-end interpreter, you know, a
conduit between the different musicians and the artist.

Like when Julian Lennon came and he felt like a fish out of
water, I sat down with Julian to calm him because he was very
nervous. That kind of ambassadorship interpreter role. I was
kind of translating for Keith, and then making Chuck relax
when we started to play, so when we were playing, he never
had a problem with the band.

JR: Chuck loved Keith, wanted Keith, but didn't want anyone else wanting Keith more than him. So even during the rehearsals, when Keith would sort of overstep Chuck and said, "Chuck, we want to do it this way," he would, like, scowl, and Chuck would just not like to be told by Keith how to do his songs.

MF: And then we had a big problem too, because I couldn't see what was going on. But I had a camera in there. And remember Bill Youdelman?

TA: Yes I do, because he and I went and recorded Chuck doing some overdubs later on in that same studio.

Chuck made a big issue if you recall, and said, "you know that's footage I'm not going to be making royalties," and he got all bent out of shape. I negotiated a deal with him that when we're rolling camera that the camera would go up and that when the camera stopped and we cut, the camera would go down. And then there was another incident.

MF: Chuck had some vintage equipment, and I wanted to borrow a pair of limiters, and I said, "Chuck can I borrow them," and he was totally cool man. "I'll pull down a rack for you." I said, "cool." He handed me the limiters and said, "seventy-five cash." "Oh, okay, well I think you should talk to Taylor or Stephanie or Tom or somebody." And Chuck says, "no, cash, man, right now."

I said, "no, you might as well keep them. It's all right, don't worry about it."

TA: I remember Chuck would always leave and disappear for an hour or two, because he was doing work on his property and the band would just run into jam sessions, which I remember watching.

MF: You know, I don't recall because I was in the truck and I wasn't involved in any drama. What I do remember though is Chuck never called Steve Jordan by his name. He kept calling him drummer, "hey drummer," the whole time, and Steve Jordan wasn't too happy about that. And he was trying somehow to make himself noticed to Chuck. But something that you guys weren't involved with was when I first walked into the rehearsal room with Keith. We saw Johnnie Johnson just playing at the piano. You know, it was Johnnie who is just such a humble guy, and we were digging what he was doing and playing and whatever. So Keith's listening, Keith is a student, you know, he's there to absorb all of this, so we hear Johnnie and he's playing and he's swinging and he's playing all this kind of big band music, and Keith turns to me and says, "son of a bitch," he says, "that's where Chuck got it from, it was piano keys." It was piano keys, Johnnie's piano and Chuck, well, he just made them into guitar licks. He took the piano licks and put them on guitar. And you know, Keith was laughing, like calling him a thief.

This led to Keith actually saying that in the interview later in the movie. Because he said, "remember, these weren't guitar keys, these were piano keys." As a result of Keith and the film, Johnnie sued Chuck and got royalties on the songs he wrote with Chuck.

TA: Joey, what was it like for you and Steve to be playing with the great Johnnie Johnson?

JS: Well, it was an amazing thing because this legendary collaboration when they played on the records. And it was unbelievably pleasant to be playing with them. It was an honor. And just so much fun because Johnnie Johnson was the sweetest, sweetest man you'll ever meet. He was just like a teddy bear and he took me under his wing, right at the start. We played and he would just start playing the blues, and I would just fall in with him and play, and everybody started playing. We had great jam sessions. At the end of the day, one of my favorite memories is him putting his arm around me and he said "Joey, my baby," and it was like really sweet and loving. So I had a really great time with Johnnie Johnson.

SUZIE PETERSEN: Well, it was the best fly on the wall experience I ever had in my life. What an incredible group of musicians and, of course, we all have memories of Chuck arguing with Keith and having no hesitation in telling him how to play his music his way. Those kind of things were tense, but also funny. And to meet these guys, especially Keith, was a great experience. And to see what sort of level-headed, totally dedicated professional Keith was. And that was true of all those guys despite the frustration of Chuck not showing up, arguing, or whatever. He could be very difficult, but they revered him and they hung in there, and I had a lot of respect for that. And then, just hearing the music, it was just wonderful. I had never heard of Robert Cray before then and certainly became a fan of his.

JA: It was so exciting. When we were in St. Louis and it was around midnight and you and Taylor were filming Chuck on stage. Eric Clapton and Terry O'Neill arrived and when they arrived, Chuck said, "I don't have a guitar" and then Keith said, "here's one." And then Eric Clapton got up on stage and they were playing, and I looked at Suzie Petersen and I said, "just pinch me. Am I dreaming this?" It was that exciting to sit five-feet away from Chuck, Eric, and Keith on that rehearsal stage performing. It was a big deal.

TA: I remember that Eric took a break and sat down next to me while Keith and Steve ran the band through another rehearsal. I asked Eric if he and Keith had played together previously and he said, "yeah, a few times, and at *The Rolling Stones Rock And*

Roll Circus television taping where we backed up John Lennon on "Yer Blues."

I remember that those rehearsals for Stephanie Bennett was kind of like being in the eye of a hurricane, because whichever direction she might have stepped out of, she was going to get caught in a "crossfire hurricane," as Keith and Mick once sang in "Jumpin' Jack Flash."

SB: I was operating at full throttle and firing on all cylinders and either putting out fires or waiting for the next blaze to ignite. And they came from all directions. "Where's fucking Chuck," "we are ready to run through 'Carol,'" "what do you mean he's on the tractor in the back forty?" "I've got Etta James standing around ready to do 'Rock And Roll Music,'" "he wants another fifty dollars to turn on the amp, what the fuck, just pay him," and on and on and on it went. Every now and then, Tom and I would retreat to the main house and sit in the kitchen to catch our breath and to have a cup of coffee. One night during one of those coffee breaks, a certain Caucasian female sat down next to us at the kitchen table and begged me to help get her out of Berry Park, before it would be too late. What the fuck. I looked at Tom who looked at me, and we both thought, "what the hell was coming next?" And so, she started to talk and after a few comments, Tom politely excused himself to go back to the rehearsals, clearly not interested in hearing or being witness to what she might say next. I won't break that confidence here, but I can tell you that what she said shook me to the bones and to this day I have never revealed what she told me to anybody. And I guess I never will, even though he is now gone.

CHAPTER SEVENTEEN
The Concert: A Night to Remember

ALL OF THE CHALLENGES *of the rehearsals and dealing with Chuck's unpredictable behavior was about one thing, and that was to put on one of, if not the greatest Chuck Berry concert that had ever been mounted. And to capture it all on film recorded on state of the art audio equipment, so that future generations would understand Chuck Berry's significance in the evolution of rock and roll music as interpreted in this film by this director. You've heard about the rehearsals and the moments of friction out at Berry Park. We have told you about that trip to Algoa Correctional Institute where the female members of our executive team came under violent attack. You've heard about the dance of making sure that Chuck Berry and Keith Richards could find a working relationship path that would stay intact, at least until the movie was in the can. But, it was all leading up to this, the mounting of two concerts at The Fox Theatre in St. Louis, Missouri, in front of packed houses of five thousand rock and roll fans. This was the real deal, and by this point, there was no turning back. The super stars of rock and roll were all in tow. The equipment and an A-level crew were standing by and the director, Taylor Hackford, was formulating his cinematic vision for how to capture these historical performances, knowing that he had one shot to do it. And I, as the lone female producer, was just waiting in the wings with baited breath for the next shoe to drop from our films' subject, Mr. Chuck Berry. Yes, the day had finally arrived and this was definitely, SHOW TIME.*

TOM ADELMAN: When you think of all of those grand old movie palaces of the early twentieth century The Fox Theatre of St. Louis, Missouri, certainly stands out. Its lush tapestry of rich colors which paint its way up and around the majestic columns and corridors leave one feeling as if they are in a scene from *The Phantom of the Opera*. If only these walls could talk. But, in 1986, they certainly were talking in the artists who graced the stage and tread those boards from night to night. And the latest addition to that stable of legendary talent would be Chuck Berry and company. Having come full circle from the young man who was not admitted entrance to see *A Tale of Two Cities*. The Fox Theatre would now host that older and more refined man in the making of his movie, which might just have been called *A Tale of Two Chucks*. The artist who could charm the pants off of anyone, to the complex and unpredictable musician that led us all through the gates of hell in trying to make *Hail! Hail! Rock 'N' Roll*. And so, now he was coming home for a rendezvous with his past.

STEPHANIE BENNETT: I think it was the hardest thing I've ever done, and when I think about it, I still realize that Chuck was probably nuts or something, there must have been something wrong with him. I don't know why, I guess because he couldn't be white that he took it out on every white person, but it's still hard to understand how anybody could not appreciate what we all did. The positive thing about it was working with Keith and Taylor and Jane Rose and Tom, and everybody all just behaved really well. So we made a film in spite of Chuck. It wasn't Chuck's understanding that he was going to do two shows. It was only supposed to be ninety minutes filmed for the documentary.

TA: What about the dressing room fiasco?

SB: Remember the whole thing with the dressing room? We got there, and there was the star's dressing room and then there was a smaller dressing room, and Chuck said, "oh, I don't need a big dressing room," and so he gave it to Keith and I said, "oh, it's a good idea, because Keith always has all these people coming in and out." So we gave Keith the big dressing room, and then Chuck said, "oh no," when he saw his dressing room, so I once again had to go to Keith and say he changed his mind...he wants that room now, and Keith was really pissed off about it. I think he was pissed off at me.

TA: Do you remember that our costume designer designed those onstage jackets for the band, and they disappeared? I remember someone said that someone stole them, but somewhere on this planet are those jackets right. We never found them or discovered where they were.

Stephanie, as you know, the entire planning of the concerts at The Fox Theatre was a complicated affair. Art direction wise, our production designer designed a large black and white poster of a younger Chuck Berry, in his glory days, which acted as a backdrop to the band. And there were different tiers of risers which the back line (drums, piano and bass) and the front line (guitars and vocals) would be positioned on.

SB: Yes, very complicated and the production designer, Kim Colfax, did a great job with the stage and that poster was glorious.

TA: Right, the scenic design complemented perfectly the beautiful and pedigree interior design of the legendary Fox Theatre, which was just one of those gorgeous old palaces, many of which have disappeared over the decades to be replaced by modern day multiplexes.

SB: I remember talking with Taylor and Oliver about making the concert very stylish and vibrant in its colors and texture.

TA: Yes, the color palate of the show was rich in vibrant tones and showed off this grand old houses' glorious past as it intersected with a late 1980s rock and roll king and his followers. It had come quite a distance along that long and winding road since those days of segregation where a young and innocent Chuck Berry was not granted admittance to the Fox Theatre so that he could watch the movie *A Tale of Two Cities.*

SB: A lot of innocence on all sides had been found and then lost again in this theater's and Chuck's simultaneous journey toward cultural closure on the night of the concerts.

A decision had been made by Taylor to actually do two shows and to film them both so we would have some alternative takes to choose from and maybe even combine some of those song performances. This turned out to be a "Tale of Two Chucks" once again.

TA: Tell me about how the decision was made to actually do two concerts instead on one.

SB: I think it was a very bad decision to do two shows. I think Taylor wanted to make sure he had a lot of options, I guess.

TA: Coverage?

SB: Yes, but I know that by doing two, they were very hard to cut together.

TA: Because there was no click track on the drummer. It was not necessarily in the same tempo.

SB: Yes, and in addition to that, Chuck lost his voice, during the whole of the second show.

TA: But how much of that losing his voice was also due to that issue of the wrong key?

MICHAEL FRONDELLI: Well, from what I understood from Taylor, when Keith listened to all of those Chess recordings, he heard them and he wrote down those keys and rehearsed the band with those keys. But, the Chess brothers, Marshall and Leonard, when they recorded Chuck, who was already a twenty-nine or thirty-year-old man, they wanted him to sound younger, so they, they recorded him and sped up the tempo, or so that he would sound like he had more of a soprano voice I think or a higher pitch, and Chuck never relayed this to Keith Richards. So Keith Richards rehearsed the band in the original keys as reflected on the albums, not knowing that the Chess guys had purposefully sped it up. Chuck never told him and from what I understood, he lost his voice because he was singing in the wrong keys. And that's one of the reasons I had to go with Bill Youdelman and dub him in Chuck's little make-shift studio. But it was probably a contributing factor of both the second show and that issue combined. Don't you think?

SB: Actually, that's good point, because he did want him to sing in a different key and, in fact, Chuck at the very opening tried to change the key of the very first song.

TA: The "Roll Over Beethoven" sequence. It's very interesting because Keith Richards had rehearsed his songs with the band and they were playing in the key of C major, and Chuck probably now remembered that "oh, that's a little bit too high for me," so that's why he went over and said, "let's change the key to B-Flat." And Keith said, "no," but Keith didn't know that maybe there was a physical issue with his voice as opposed to just a random act of defiance, in terms of just I want to do it in the key of F and not the key of G, you know. All the songs have different keys. They weren't necessarily all E or G or.

KEITH RICHARDS: In the middle of "Roll Over Beethoven" at the Fox Theatre, Chuck comes up to me in the solo and says, "after this chorus, we're going to change the key from…we're in C to B-Flat." And, I said "no." I did a double take. I don't think many people would say no to Chuck. Even when it's going great, he won't leave it alone. He'll come in and there's the potential to screw it up, and, it's just him. I don't think he's…he's not malicious or vicious or designed. He's just him and you just gotta be…when you're working with Chuck, you got to be prepared for anything, any time. We rehearsed for ten days. This goes with this song, piano solo here, and then you get onstage and boom out the window, wing it. Ah, everybody's looking at me onstage and totally different arrangement, some of them in different keys, and, ah, I just looked at them and said, "wing it, boys."

JANE ROSE: Keith came off the stage. There were these nine or ten cameras, Taylor was on the side just waiting to do the switching and everything, and Keith came off the stage, he wants to change the key to B-flat, I mean, I couldn't…Keith was there to my right actually. Because they were playing on stage, but I think that Keith really went into it with the purest of hearts and intentions. He wanted this to be really good for Chuck. I don't think he had any other motive than to do as pure as he could possibly do it for him.

STEVE JORDAN: Chuck wanted to change key, because he couldn't hit those notes, and Keith didn't want to change the key because it would have been, I mean, I don't doubt that the rest of the band would have changed the key, but, you know, to avoid any kind of problems, Keith elected not to change anything. I mean, keep doing it in one key, he wasn't going to be trying to search to, you know, to play it on stage in a new key. But obviously, Chuck wanted to change the key, because his voice wasn't great. Now the reason why his voice wasn't great was at the last rehearsal before the show when we were supposed to be rehearsing, Chuck went and took a gig at the Ohio State Fair and he wasn't supposed to do that. He took the gig and blew his voice out, so come show time, he's got like half of his voice. That's why we had to dub half of the vocals in the film. We had to fly Chuck to New York, and we sat with Chuck in a room at Giant Sound in New York City, and he had to do half of the vocals if not more again because he had no voice... he was hoarse.

TA: You know there has been this theory and maybe you can confirm or not confirm this, that one of the reasons Chuck blew his voice out, besides the Ohio State Fair show was because in the original recordings, they had recorded him in a different key or sped up the recordings, and he never told any of you guys that and you were rehearsing in keys that were on the record. Is there any truth to that?

SJ: You know something. I had never heard, but, let me tell you something not only is that quite plausible, but quite probable, and I only know this from working and when you go back to some of those records. Now I have to check the keys on some of them, because if they ended up being in guitar keys, well that's the reason why, because they were sped up. I know that from my experience when I worked on the Sly and the Family Stone remix album; I got the original tapes. And came to find out Sly and the Family Stone had cut a lot of their stuff in piano keys, in E-Flat and stuff like that because Sly was primarily a piano player, organ player, and that's where he wrote them. So if you listen to some of the songs, if you listen to some of the big hits like "Everyday People," "Sing A Simple Song," music like that—"Sing A Simple Song" in particular—when you hear "Roll Sister Roll," she sounds like Minnie Mouse, you know, she's got this voice, but they recorded a lot of stuff a half step lower, so she sounds more like Etta James in real life. So if you listen to those records, they're all sped up. They're like freeze-dried records, and I tell you, if they had been released in the original key, they would not have been hits. They were sped up to the right tempo, and made more buoyant in the higher key to make it more pop accessible, and basically not a flat key, you know, so it made it more accessible to the general public. It was just happier. It was happier music. It wasn't as blues oriented, you see. And so if Sly Stone did it, and I'm not surprised at all by the revelation of that, they did that at Chess. It doesn't surprise me at all. It makes total sense actually.

TA: Wasn't Chuck about thirty years old already when he was recording things like "School Days." They wanted to make him sound younger or something like that.

SJ: Well, I don't know if that was the reason. I have no idea, but as far as we didn't have software at the time where you could raise the key and keep the same tempo or change the tempo and keep the same key. Once you sped something up, the key went up and the tempo went up. So there were probably two things involved you know, the tempo and the key.

TA: Did the concerts more or less unfold musically the way that you guys planned them in the rehearsals?

SJ: Musically, I think we came out satisfactory. Ah, the performance of "Rock and Roll Music." The very first time we did it, and I don't think its on camera. I think its lost. If you weren't there, you missed it. But the very first time that Etta James walked on stage at Wentzville and we did "Rock and Roll Music," it was unreal, and we just tried to get it to feel like that again and we never did. It was an incredible, incredible performance. The vocal was incredible…everything was incredible.

SB: Maybe if Chuck had interacted more with Keith, the hoarse voice wouldn't have been an issue. I mean, they barely spoke to each other. So the problem was there was no communication going on there, you know.

TA: It's true. He was so arrogant in his behavior and disrespectful of the musical director and all those great artists at that concert. But these guys were so professional, and they knew who they were and what they were doing at The Fox Theatre. As Keith said in his interview, "I knew what I was getting into."

Dick Allen had been Chuck's personal appearance agent from those very early days in the 1950s and had been with him ever since. He was brought to St. Louis to be at those concerts, probably to run interference between Chuck and the production team, and run interference he did. When Taylor decided that he wanted to have two shows performed and filmed, this came as a surprise to Chuck, and basically to everybody else.

DICK ALLEN: Well, as you know, I was not the agent on the film; although, I did represent Chuck in all his personal appearances, but I wasn't on this particular job. I don't know if there was an agent. I forget the reason I was asked to come to St. Louis the day before the concert. But I came to St. Louis anyway and someone picked me up and took me out to Berry Park. I saw the end of rehearsal, and I went to the show the next day. Now at the show, this is where the trouble started. Chuck was all set to do the show and everything was going fine. Taylor then wanted a second show, so he could take the best of both shoots and combine them to make the movie that he finally made. So no one had ever cleared this with Chuck Berry to do it twice. So, I'm in the dressing room with Chuck, and he suddenly says, "Dick how much are they paying me for the second show?" And I said, "I don't know, I didn't make the deal." So he said, "well find out." So I then left his dressing room and went to the room wherever Taylor and Stephanie were and told them what Chuck's request was. They said "no, there's no money. We're just doing this to get the best show for him." I said, "he's going to want money." They said, "no, no, no, we just want to have the best show." I went back to Chuck and told him that. He said, "No. No second show unless I get paid." And so, I went and spent a number of trips going back and forth. They finally got some money together. I think even taken out of the the popcorn stand vendor. And so, Chuck finally did the second show. And, of course, Taylor's not happy and Chuck is implacable. I wasn't there in any official capacity. Somebody had to fly me there, and it wasn't Chuck because Chuck is cheap. So I don't know who had me come to St. Louis, but, I was there, and Chuck is always happy to use anybody. Especially because we had been together for decades. So in any case, they finally did the second show, not much audience was left. I remember Linda Ronstadt left annoyed.

TA: You know it's funny when you think about it, you flew in kind of not knowing you were coming in a day before, and you may have saved the entire movie by acting as kind of the ambassador between Taylor, Stephanie, and Chuck.

DA: It's possible. I know it helps with a tough guy and very implacable and very, very stubborn. When he made up his mind about something, that was it. The other thing is, as you know, he has nobody: no manager, no road manager, no nothing. So somehow that's why I landed in the middle.

SB: So it was kind of how much. And, of course, it was Saturday, the banks are closed. I didn't have any checks. He didn't want a check, he wanted cash, so we basically rounded up all the cash from the safe. I think, I don't know how much was in there at the end of the day, but I do remember that it was put into a brown paper bag. It was cash, and I do remember that it was the last night and it was the first time that I actually told him what I thought of him. I guess because at that point I didn't care if he went on or not. It was just such a nightmare, and I threw the money across the dressing room and I don't remember exactly what I said, but it was like, "you don't deserve this. All these people mean nothing to you," blah, blah, blah, but ultimately, I mean, in a way the film never lies and I think the film shows who Chuck really is.

JR: When he said, "time is up," time was up. "I'm going unless you bring me a brown paper bag." You know the music was no longer a priority. He didn't care about it. I think he lost the passion or the love of what he did to make it perfect as a poet. You'd think he would want everything to be perfect. You'd think he really wanted it to be great, and I think this is where he had a problem with Keith, in that Keith was in charge of what he did and he had a hard time with that. It was a yin and yang thing. He loved it and he hated it.

SB: It was like a chip that was built into him, like a kneejerk thing, he had to react. I kept saying to myself, "why don't you care about these people being here. Why don't you care about this film? Why don't you care about Taylor or Keith?" It was like he wouldn't allow himself the enjoyment of it. It had to be more money; the only thing that gave him any sense of comfort was money. It was just extraordinary.

HELEN MIRREN: Yes, that was clear. That was simple, direct, straightforward. A load of cash in a suitcase. There's no arguing with it. You know, it's a simple, straightforward thing.

TAYLOR HACKFORD: That night was a crazy, crazy night at the Fox Theatre, because number one, Chuck had shown up late. Number two, he's sick and losing his voice. Of all the nights that he should have full voice, he's got five thousand people coming to one show; five thousand people coming to the second show. He's got ten thousand people, and he really didn't care about the people from St. Louis. People had flown in from all over the world to be there. He's got no voice. He goes up on the stage and Keith is trying to rehearse this band. They've got everything set, and, of course, that's where it began. Once the concert began, everything started to fly out the window. I think that actually Chuck was beginning to realize, "oh my God I'm here and I've got five thousand people out there yelling and screaming." And of course, I'm shooting 35mm film. That means I only have three songs per roll of film. I have ten cameras, so at the end of each, at the end of a three song cycle, we've got to stop filming and reload. In the process, I gave him a breather, except Johnnie Johnson would play these boogie runs, and Steve Jordan has a great description of what happened and how exhausting these things were.

SJ: In between the switching of the reels, the crowd was there and we had to entertain them. Well Johnnie was compelled to burst into the fastest shuffle known to man. Now we got a long show ahead of us and another one afterward. You know, this is kind of what we're looking at here. And the first time he broke into it, the crowd loves it, they get into it. Okay, great. You know, seven minutes, we're breaking in at ten-minute shuffles, ten, I mean everybody's soloing. Okay, that happens once. They play another three tunes, get back into the swing of the show. Gotta switch again. Well, this goes on for about four or five times. I am wiped out. He is wiping me out, and he has affectionately named me Dum Dum. So he would come up, "hey, Dum Dum, here we go." And, he wore me out. He completely wore...I was never so tired before or ever after a show. All I wanted to do after this whole night was over was drink milk. That's all I wanted to do. Everybody's drinking champagne, and Keith's got his bottle of bourbon and milk, that was it. I may have been lactose intolerant, but it wasn't affecting me that night.

TH: The audience was part of the process. The first concert was eventful. There were moments where you're listening and going, God he's got no voice, what are we going to do? Are we going to have to loop this? But I'm shooting and I'm bound and determined to get it. The guests are on. There was something about a live show, because Chuck Berry was flying by the seat of his pants. All the performers knew it. They knew he didn't have a voice. How would he respond? You know how he responded? Like Chuck Berry. He is the guy who started it all.

I believe that during his performance he kind of fell back on that thing, well this is a movie. "It is about me. No matter what, I still do this better than anybody, so I'm going to do it. I don't even have to have a voice. I'm going to kill this thing. This is the stuff I wrote. The stuff I came up with. The stuff I invented. It's still mine and it'll always be mine."

TA: Curt, when you saw that there was going to be two performances, were you concerned that there might be lyrical differences or issues and tempo changes, and you were going to have to possibly cut songs from two performances from both shows together?

CURT SOBEL: I could tell that on some songs, it seemed like he had forgotten the lyrics or mixing up the lyrics. Something was not quite right with the lyrics. But it didn't matter to the performance. The audience didn't know, but I kept thinking, well, that's going to be tough on close shots of his face, because if he's not singing the right lyrics or not getting it right, they're going to have to stay on one shot. Something was happening. I didn't quite understand what was going on.

TH: During the first concert, he wasn't doing so well on lyrics, so in between concerts we realized that we better get some cue cards for the second show.

CS: We got Chuck singing these lyrics and he did use the cue cards. He was such a professional that it didn't matter to him, he knew he needed the help. He read the cue cards, but you couldn't tell. The audience didn't seem to be able to tell, because his enthusiasm, and the sweat, and the love of this music was there both in the musicians and in Chuck, and so it was fantastic. The other complication though with the second concert was that he'd been through a first concert screaming out lyrics, whatever words they were. And here we are and his voice was rather hoarse the second concert, so now the challenge is we got him singing the words but his voice is almost lost. Now we're stuck with a vocal that is not the best vocal that you'd want out of Chuck. So in post when we came back to Los Angles, we're editing the picture, Chuck was an absolute professional, great looper. We brought him in to resing a lot of those verses for the songs in a better, stronger voice, and in some of those songs, that's what's used in the final print.

SB: At the Fox Theatre in St. Louis, Chuck had indeed developed sort of a scratchy voice, but it turned out to be much worse than we imagined.

TA: The concert itself was a daunting and challenging event to pull off creatively and musically, but so was the approach for the filming of the performances. The director of photography, Oliver Stapleton.

OLIVER STAPLETON: I was slightly puzzled about why he wanted quite so many cameras, because I wasn't used to that. I was used to the economic, kind of low-budget England type of cinema, so for me to shoot in concert with three cameras was quite a lot, so, to shoot the concert with five/six/seven…I can't remember how many there were, but there were a lot. To me, that was a real extravagance. So my task was really to make sure that they all had the right lenses, the right people, they worked, and then we sorted out together where they should go, and I didn't have any problem with that. Taylor and I worked together again last year, which was thirty something years later, and we just fell right back into a good and easy relationship. I find him, his notions of where the cameras go and what they should do, to be very clear. It's not what some directors do, a mystery sometimes and you have to second guess what on earth they're talking about. With Taylor, he's a good communicator and it's pretty clear what he wants. With the 35mm film, the idea was to light the concert very stylishly and be able to shoot very highly quality 35mm, so that the concert would really stand out in quality, as away from the documentary, so the two things would feel completely different. We also used a Louma crane for the concert footage, which was a very unusual remote crane, and at the time was really at its very beginning of its use in the USA, so much so that I actually couldn't find anybody to operate it, so I had to do that myself. The basic system that you employ when you shoot a concert with the Louma is that Taylor would sit with all his monitors. He had a headset to me and to the other operators, and then I had a headset not just to him, but also to the grip, who was on my crane, so basically, we just improvised lots of moves as we were shooting and I would be constantly speaking to the grips on the crane and saying, okay and up, left, right, and down, and all that stuff, and then Taylor would occasionally make some comment from the monitors if he saw something he particularly wanted or wasn't getting, you know? Then he'd yell out at this camera operator or that camera operator, etc. The rather spectacular thing that did happen was that during one song my crane stopped moving. When I was giving directions into the headphones and the crane wasn't moving, I was questioning what's going on, what's happening, and the crane had come down to the ground and the grip said to me, "I'm having dinner." I promise you, this is true and he just sat there on the box eating a sandwich during the concert, and stopped shooting. I think it was because we obviously hadn't broken the crew for a very, very long time and no one had seen fit to speak to him about it. So, he just decided to have his sandwich, and we stopped shooting for a few minutes and then when he finished he said, "okay, ready."

TA: It was a night to remember, but we all got through it. But the party wasn't over yet. Now we were going to embark on the postproduction process back in Los Angeles, which would bring on it's own new set of Chuck Berry dramas.

CHAPTER EIGHTEEN
Chuck's House in LA:
Full of Surprises

POSTPRODUCTION: *Life in another Chuck Berry house and putting a voice to the show*

STEPHANIE BENNETT: My company, Delilah Films, was based on the East Coast, in Westport, Connecticut. Taylor Hackford was living and working in LA, so the postproduction would be done there. It was decided to rent a place there so at least Tom Adelman, my line producer for the movie, who was also in charge of the post work, would have somewhere to stay. On hearing we were doing this, Chuck offered his house in LA. We mistakenly thought it was free, but no, nothing with Chuck was free. It was $2,000 a month rent, please, and in cash. The Bronson Avenue property was the only circular lot with a moth-eaten deer in the front yard. Our first visit to the house was like walking into something out of the seventies— shag pile orange carpets, green velvet couches, and dust so thick you could grab it by the handful. In the main room was a weird sculpture of a woman with her breasts and knees supporting the glass table. I covered it up when I had children visit. We discovered that he had cameras in the main bedroom and, while I was away, he told my husband where the record switch was if he had any visitors, wink wink.

TOM ADELMAN: I then had to make the transition from production into postproduction. So we needed a place for me to stay so I could work with Taylor Hackford on this phase of the movie. Now as it turned out, Chuck Berry happened to own a house in Hollywood at the top of Bronson Avenue, just north of Franklin. It was a bit unique as it sat on the only circular acre in Los Angeles. When Chuck got wind of the fact that I would be needing a place to stay during postproduction, he generously offered the use of his home as a place for me to live in and operate from. Of course, as there usually was with Chuck, there was a price to pay. And so, he worked out a deal with Stephanie Bennett to rent the entire house out for $2,000 a month. As Chuck would say, "That's a sweet deal, Stephanie, but, as you know, there is always a way to lower the price."

Of course Stephanie, who by this time was on to Chuck, agreed to pay the monthly stipend with no G-strings attached, if you will. And so, I moved into Chuck's house on Bronson Avenue.

SB: If I had previously refused to play Chuck's little game in order to save $30,000.00, there certainly was no possibility that I was going to step over that line in the sand for $2,000.00. Sorry Chucky, but you'll have to look elsewhere for additional conquests. Now, Tom was a bit hesitant about this because we had all just gone to hell and back on a "Downbound Train" with Chuck (Casey Jones) Berry as the train engineer. So I looked at Tom and said, "I'm sure everything will be just fine, and anyway, "it's for the cause."

TA: Stephanie and I met Chuck at the house so he could show me the place and let me know where I could sleep and what rooms I should stay out of and what not to touch. When you walked in, you got the sense that you were walking into a museum, as there was a strange collage of furniture, rugs, and carpeting, and artwork on the walls that must have spanned five decades and had no sense of interior decoration continuity. Yes, a real museum, except that this was no ordinary museum. This was more like the Ripley's Museum of Believe It or Not. This was something else, this was it's own thing, and it read Chuck Berry in every nook and cranny. When you first walked into the house on Bronson Avenue, right smack in the middle of the living room, was this strange coffee table with a glass top. This was an unusual table as it was held up by a naked bronzed woman sculpture underneath, whose knees and arms supported the heavy glass surface. Chuck switched the table on and all of a sudden hot golden oil started dripping down each part of the woman's body that was connected to the glass surface and landing in little drain mechanisms that would circulate the oil back again for further distribution through the sculptures body.

SB: That table basically said everything about Chuck and frankly, neither of us were too surprised. Anyway, I dropped Tom off with his bags and left him in his new residence. I remember as I was driving away, seeing Tom watching me from the open door with a look of pleading for me to take him with me. But, as we all know, the show must go on. "Don't worry, Tom, I'll visit often."

TA: So Stephanie left and I was left alone in this house with Chuck Berry who made it clear what the rules of the house were. "Don't touch this, stay away from that room. Don't even think about opening that door," and on and on and on. He showed me the room I would stay in and so, I dropped my gear in there and walked Chuck out to the driveway where he jumped into his vehicle, rolled down the window, and looked at me with that CB smile and said, "I'll be watching, and remember, no girls." "WHAT?" Well, we'll see about that,

I thought to myself. Chuck Berry telling me no girls in his house? I couldn't even invite a girl over, ever? This guy had girls stashed in every corner of the USA and he was telling me I could not even have a normal relationship? Anyway, everyday I would drive over to the cutting rooms where Lisa Day, our main editor, would be sitting with Taylor Hackford cutting Super 16mm documentary footage and discussing scenes and order of sequences. We also had an editing room set up just to cut the songs from the concert performance and Paul Justman was behind the Steenbeck flatbed film editing system attacking those performances. So Taylor Hackford would swing between both editing suites directing the assembly. I used to sit at night at this little table in the kitchen right by the main entrance to the house and the car park. There was a swimming pool and a tennis court. I would sit there and work on postproduction. And every now and then, at night, Chuck Berry would just show up in one of his Cadillacs and walk in. He would see me sitting there and he would just sit down directly in front of me. I would say, "Hi Chuck, how's it going?" And he would just stare at me and not respond or even say a word. He would just stare me down. And so, I would try to focus on my work, and every so often, glance up at him and he would still be staring at me. And this would go on for maybe an hour, maybe an hour and a half. Then, eventually, he would stand up, go into some hidden dark corner of the house, behind closed doors, and I would not see him again for maybe an hour or two. Then he would come out, look over at me, and then just split, and that was it, until the next time he happened to pop on by for a visit. As time went by, I got a bit more comfortable in that house. Being a guy from NYC, I really didn't know many people in LA, other than the postproduction team. So I often found myself alone on a

Friday night or over the weekend. There was a pretty famous liquor store down the street from Chuck's house and every so often on weekends, I would wander down there to purchase a bottle of red wine, or some rose champagne, or something to just unwind after a tough week on the production. Well, one night, the liquor store was closed for some reason, and so I went back to the house and flicked on the large television to see what was on. But I distinctly recall really feeling a bit thirsty for a glass of wine. Well, I thought, this guy must have a few bottles of anything stashed away somewhere in this pad? So, I looked around, open this cabinet...he never mentioned to stay away from that one. Nothing in the fridge, what's in there, nothing. Let me open this and wham, sitting directly in front of me was a large three level glass shelf with at least five thousand little bottles of liquor that he kept from decades of flights going from here to there. You know, those little liquor bottles that you get on airplanes? Brandy, liquors, Johnny Walker Black or Red, Chivas Regal. He had them all from some forty years of flights. In the back, I spotted a small mini bottle of Veuve Cliquot champagne. This bottle was way in the back, maybe six or seven layers deep into the shelf. There were hundreds if not thousands of little bottles in front of it. So, I thought, what the hell, just go for it. And so, I took the bottle, put it on ice and then enjoyed the few sips of champagne that it contained and that more or less quenched my thirst for alcohol, as I was never much of a drinker. A few weeks went by and business as usual and than, one night, I was sitting at that kitchen table, doing my work as usual, and there he is, driving up in a different Cadillac. Chuck comes in and I say, "hi," and I think he may have acknowledged me this time with a quick wink and a nod. And he disappeared back into the private quarters of his house. And then, all of a sudden, all hell broke loose. Chuck came tearing into the kitchen, hopping mad. "Who told you that you could drink from my liquor cellar? This was not part of the deal with Stephanie and my liquor is not included in the rent. Where is she and what's her number?" I couldn't believe it. I had forgotten all about that one little mini bottle amongst literally thousands of other little bottles from weeks ago. But this guy walked into that house, opened up that cabinet and immediately spotted that one little bottle was missing. I forget how it got worked out, and I have no doubt that what it must have cost Stephanie Bennett for that little mini bottle of champagne. I probably could have run out and purchased a case of Crystal for the same ransom. But you can be sure, from that moment on, I was hesitant about even having a glass of water from Chuck's faucet. Now, Chuck's house had a lot of kitchen appliances in it and other equipment, such as his washing machine. And most of this equipment showed wear and tear over the ages and sometimes things would not work properly. And that reminds me of one particular story involving Stephanie Bennett's husband, Jim Mervis.

JIM MERVIS: Some of us, at one time or another were living in Chuck's house in Hollywood during part of the making of the film, and Chuck would show up the first Saturday of every month to collect the rent in cash. Naturally, he used to arrive with his Samsonite attaché case. And in the attaché case, he always had the same items. He had six or seven white envelopes for collecting the cash from different houses that he owned and rented out, always in cash. He also had a biography of Albert Einstein, which he told me he was reading slowly and he admired Einstein. Anyway, we were there for a while and one day as things do happen, the washing machine broke down. So I figured I'll just call the Sears repairman and get it fixed, but Chuck was so finicky about who was allowed in the house and things like that, I figured I better call him. So I called him and I said, "Chuck, I'm going to get the washing machine fixed. It's just gone dead, and I know a little bit about electrical things, and I think something's blown out and it needs to be repaired. I just wanted to let you know." He says, "oh no, no, he…you can't let the Sears repairman in the house. I'm going to be there Saturday. I'll fix it." I said, "Chuck you're a great songwriter. You're a great musician. You don't have to be a great repairman also. Let me call the Sears repairman." He said, "no, you may not call the Sears repairman." Okay, so that Saturday morning Chuck arrives and he's got his attaché case and he's got his envelopes and he's got the biography of Einstein and he's also got a screwdriver, a pair of pliers, and a hammer. So there's this laundry room and there's water all over the floor because, basically, in addition to stopping, it sprung a leak somewhere, and there's a good inch of water on the floor in this room. And I said, "Chuck we've got to clean out the water." "Oh no…I don't have time. I got to fix this and I know exactly what to do." So he goes in and he proceeds to rip the back off of the washing machine control panel. He takes out the screwdriver and his pliers and tries to jump start it like it's a car and I said, "Chuck, let me help you." And Stephanie's standing there, and she grabs me and says, "you are not walking into that water-flooded room." But he just kept on and seriously there was this question of if he tries to jump start this and he's standing in a puddle of water, he could die. He could kill himself. And we're just watching and watching and suddenly there's this huge spark and sure enough Chuck Berry gets thrown across the room and gets stopped by the wall. He lands on his ass in the water and for a split second he doesn't look like he's conscious, but then his eyes open, he looks up and says, "see, I told you I could start it." And it turned over. It turned over once or twice and then died again. But, he was very proud of himself. Dusted himself off, wiped himself off. We all breathed a sigh of relief. I started to understand that he respects these little accomplishments. So, I said, "Chuck you know, you told us that when we first occupied the house, do not even try using the microwave as it was broken." "Don't worry about it. I might replace it at some point in time." I was in the kitchen and he was drying himself off. I said, "Chuck you know, I actually fixed the microwave." He said, "you fixed the microwave. I don't believe it." So, he goes and he turns it on and he puts something in, and it works. So he looks at me and says, "you are the captain. I'm going to call you Captain from now on." And this was important. This was a big move, because he was the captain, he wore a captain's hat all the time. So for him to call me Captain was like, wow…we're bros.

TA: My recollection is that he trusted you.

JM: What I didn't tell him is that there is a compartment on the back of the microwave that you unscrew and you change the fuse. That's all that had to be done. But I went up several levels of respect in his eyes. I didn't realize what this meant for a while, and it wasn't until Stephanie was out on the road that he gives me a call, and I'm still in Hollywood and staying in the house and doing some other work. And he calls me up and he says, "Jim, I want you to know where the switch is to turn on the cameras." I said, "Chuck what are you talking about." He says, "I have cameras in the bedroom behind the left-hand red curtain, there's a switch, so if you have any other women out there while Stephanie's away, you have to share it with me." "Really?" "Yeah, yeah, its important." So that was another insight into fun loving Captain Chuck.

TA: Did you happen to, after hearing that story, examine his video collection?

JM: No, but I did actually look behind the curtain and there was a switch. I never took him up on his suggestion though.

TA: After hearing about Chuck's cameras in the bedrooms, I suddenly for some reason lost any interest in inviting any girlfriends over for a visit. I can only say thank heavens there was no YouTube in those days.

CHAPTER NINETEEN
Mixing it up with Chuck

"Mixing it Up with Chuck"
—The Sound Mix

Now the sound mix *on a film, especially a film about music, is a critical element in the overall presentation of the finished product. All too often in the movie industry, the emphasis on and the significance of getting the mix right is lost in the shuffle of picture editing, looping, pick-up shots, and everything else. A less than stellar sound mix can detract from the overall experience of seeing a movie and significantly impact the reviews and, in general, critical acclaim among the public and the industry. Now toss into the gumbo of filmmaking the fact that we were dealing with the master mixer, shake-up artist himself, Chuck Berry, a wonderful director in Taylor Hackford, and a legendary world-famous rock and roller in the person of Keith Richards, and you have set a table with a potential recipe for disaster. A director is focused on dramatic arcs and storytelling, and a music producer just wants to get the music and sound as authentically correct as possible. And sometimes these two visions do not complement each other. This can be evidenced by a Taylor Hackford and Keith Richards confrontation that occurred during the final sound mix, but we'll get back to that little dust up outside of the sound facility later. While we were preparing for the movie sound mix, we were also getting the cues ready for the soundtrack release of* Hail! Hail! Rock 'N' Roll.

A lot of this work would take place at the legendary Electric Lady Studios on Eighth Street in NYC's famed Village.

TOM ADELMAN: At some point during postproduction of the movie, I spent a week in New York with Keith and Chuck doing overdubs and mixing what would become the movie's soundtrack release. This was a very interesting week because different buddies of Keith would swing by to say hello and hang out for a while. Mick Taylor came by, Patty Scialfa (Bruce Springsteen's wife) came by, and others. Michael Frondelli, the movie's main sound engineer was tied up on another album at the time, so he brought in the great Don Wershba to run the board.

MICHAEL FRONDELLI: What happened was that I had another record I was involved with. So I hired another engineer named Don Wershba, and I told Don, "Chuck's coming to New York for two days. He's got to overdub these vocals. We've got to get these. So could you fill in for me?" And Don is a sweet guy, and he's still around and he works for Solid State Logic. So Don came in and he had Chuck for two days, and he called me up afterward and told me what happened, and that he was great the first day and the second day he was a nightmare.

TA: Yeah, I remember that. Chuck on day two fell into his old routine of "mixing it up" with the producers and so, that particular night, time moved slowly. And there was quite a bit of set-ups between takes as well. One night, maybe around 11:00 p.m. or so, I was sitting in the client's lounge and having a coffee and the television was on playing *The Twilight Zone*. Keith Richards walks in and sits down and he had an apple in his hand. He used to carry about a six- or seven-inch butterfly gravity knife in his boot, which he snapped open and started carving up the apple with and eating pieces off of the knife.

The Twilight Zone episode ends and the next thing you know, a documentary on The Beatles pops up on the television. So here I am, sitting there watching Keith Richards checking out a documentary on the other great British invasion band. And I remember after a while that Keith said, "The thing about those guys were those vocal harmonies and some great song writing. McCartney and Lennon were lucky that they found each other." And I remember thinking, "Yeah, but how about how great it is that you and Mick found each other too," but, of course, I didn't say anything. Another memorable story was that my best friend in high school in New York, where I grew up, was William Linden. I had been living in LA, but as I was going to be back in NYC for a week at Electric Lady, I invited Billy to come and sit in at Electric Lady and hang out. Of course, I wanted to introduce my best friend to Keith and that made me kind of proud. Anyway, Billy shows up and he walks up the flight of stairs leading to the control room. He sees Keith Richards sitting next to me. So I say, "Hi, Billy, Keith, this is my best friend Billy Linden, Billy, meet Keith." Billy stood there for a moment, his eyes wide as a full moon, and all of a sudden Keith Richards says, "Tom, what the hell is wrong with you, get on up and give your friend Billy a seat." So I got up and Billy sat down in my seat next to Keith Richards. It was a great moment, which neither Billy or I ever forgot, and in fact we still laugh about it. After about an hour, Keith handed Billy some cash and asked him to go on out and pick up some Jack Daniels and a few six packs of beer. But it was great to be able to share this kind of an experience with your best high school mate.

As the movie was being edited, simultaneously, we were doing audio premixes for the movie itself at studios around Hollywood...Larabee Sound and Sunset Sound. Robert Schaper, a great mixer, was brought in to supervise these premixes. One day at Sunset Sound, I was walking back to the studio after having worked something out with the studio manager, and I walked by this lone figure with a hoodie covering his face sitting on one of the benches writing something into a notebook. As I walked by, he looked up, and lo and behold, I'm eye to eye with Bob Dylan. So I said hello and he asked me what I was doing at Sunset Sound. And I told Dylan we were doing sound mixes for the Chuck Berry movie, and he asked me if he could come in and listen and watch for a while. So of course, I said yes, and so Bob and I walked back to the studio together and he sat down and watched the mix for about an hour or so. And that was a thrill for me, having always been a huge Dylan fan.

These sessions were late night affairs and one night at Larabee Sound we were getting near the completion of the movie and the team was in a kind of a festive mood, and the usual assortment of refreshments were on hand, if you know what I mean. Taylor, and Helen, and Keith, and Jane were there and Stephanie and I were there. And a who's who of famous musicians would come by to visit Keith. Waddy Wachtel, the great guitar player came by, I think Ronnie Wood, Levon Helm (from The Band), and Harry Dean Stanton paid a visit and another guest one evening was Tom Waits. One night the "team" was having a productive mixing session and then all of a sudden there was a technical snafu and bang... downtime. This must have been about 1:00 a.m. or 2:00 a.m. The downtime lasted over an hour. So Keith Richards wanders into the studio and sits down at the Steinway grand piano and starts playing some blues and then he breaks into, "The Nearness of You," a song from 1938, composed by Hoagy Carmichael. Keith is singing softly, and Helen Mirren walks in and stands by the piano and starts to accompany Keith on vocals. By this time of the morning, everybody was feeling quite relaxed and "kissing the sky," if you will. Anyway, Keith is playing and Helen continues to sing, and he starts to play a bit louder and Helen started to vocalize a bit louder, and this went on with both instruments rising in their respective volumes and all of a sudden, Keith Richards pulls out a six or seven inch butterfly gravity knife from his boot, flips it open, and sticks it on the piano and says, "Helen, my dear, you are a lovely actress and I love your work, but if you don't stop singing, I'm going to cut your throat from ear to ear." And that was that. Helen refrained from accompanying Keith any further and Keith continued to play little bluesy passages.

One of my duties as Line Producer during these mixes was to pick up and drive Keith Richards back and forth most every day and night to the Chateau Marmont Hotel on Sunset Boulevard. It wasn't that far between these two places, but I was always a bit nervous being the guy behind the wheel with one of the main Rolling Stones as my passenger riding shotgun. What if I got into a deadly accident and that was the end of The Rolling Stones? So I probably drove at five miles an hour. We used to leave the studio and drive north on Doheny Drive. I remember Keith noted one night that "Ronnie Wood always told me that if you need to get somewhere in LA, just head north on Doheny." Anyway, one morning, maybe about three a.m. we had wrapped, and so Keith and I jumped into my car. I think it may have been a Volvo, if I remember, and we headed north up Doheny to Sunset and then turned east toward The Chateau Marmont. Well, we got to the hotel and for some reason the front doors were locked, and nobody was at reception. Maybe at three in the morning, whomever was on duty figured nobody would be coming in at that hour and went to the restroom or something. Anyway, Keith

Richards was locked out of the hotel. There was a high gate that encompassed the Chateau and it was locked as well. But if you could get inside it, one could enter into the hotel through the back of the hotel. So, all of a sudden, Keith Richards starts scaling the gate, it must have been about nine or ten feet high, and he climbed over the gate and he was in. Keith waved good night and that was it.

STEPHANIE BENNETT: It soon became apparent that there really was going to be a problem with Chuck's voice cracking at the concert. So Taylor determined that we were going to need to do some over dubbing of Chuck on a portion of the songs.

TA: I found out about an audio engineer named Billy Youdelman. Taylor wanted Chuck to come to Los Angeles so we could do the dubbing, but Chuck refused. So it was determined that Billy and I would fly to Wentzville, Missouri, and do the voice replacement at Chuck's studio at Berry Park. Armed with ¾ inch video tapes of each song and audio tapes to record on, Billy and I made our way to Missouri. We arrived for day one at Berry Park and this was to be a scout and an opportunity for Billy to examine Chuck's twenty-four track recording board and other equipment. I distinctly remember that when I asked Billy what he thought, he said, "well, I think I can make it work, but we cannot use tracks twenty-three or twenty-four" and I asked why not. And Billy said, "because it looked like some mice had eaten through the wiring." So that was more or less what we were dealing with at Chuck's home studio. So we started working the next day and the thing that was most incredible was that Chuck was a genius at lipsynching to those songs. Both Billy and I couldn't believe how accurate he was. He was nearly flawless and maybe needed at the most three takes for any given cue. Between set-ups and during downtime, Chuck would disappear, the way he had during the rehearsals for the concert, and so Billy and I would bring our lunch every day and just sit outside on the property and take a break. For those three or four days, we stayed at a nearby Missouri Bed and Breakfast just off the main highway to Wentzville. Finally, when we wrapped, we thanked Chuck, said our good-byes, and headed on back to Los Angeles with the tapes. I recall as we drove away from Berry Park looking back and seeing Chuck standing there with this bandana tied around his head and waving good-bye.

The next phase of the postproduction process and the final part was the sound mix, or what we in the industry call the sound rerecord phase. This includes Foley work. Foley work is where you bring in loop groups to make things like audience sounds and footsteps, glasses clinking against each other during a toast and other atmospheric sounds that might not have been picked up properly during the actual production. And following Foley work would be the final mix.

TA: Donald O. Mitchell, Kevin O'Connell, and Rick Kline was a legendary mixing team who worked out of Glen Glenn/Todd-A-O Studios in Los Angeles. This team of mixers had been involved with big films in the past and were some of the best in the business. And so the process started.

Usually, when producers and the director show up to start the sound mix, there is always morning craft service available where the producers sit. This normally includes orange juice, bagels, muffins, fruit, and other typical morning breakfast items. This is what was laid out for consumption on day one when Keith Richards showed up. But, starting on day two, those assorted delicacies had evolved into bottles of Jack Daniels, assorted fine wines, beers, and buckets of ice. I must say that I don't remember any of us complaining. I believe there were about three weeks of sound mixing and every day was an adventure. Carlton Kaller was a music editor, and I remember that Carl became pretty palsy with Keith Richards. Carl's job was to trouble shoot any technical sync issues that might arise during the final mix portion of the operation and to be able to correct any issues on the spot that might pop-up. In those days, all of the audio elements were on 35mm mag track tape, which were all threaded on individual machines on the floor above the mixing theater stage. These elements included all of the dialogue, sound effects, as well as all of the individual music tracks. On the last day of the mix, prior to what they called in those days, the print mastering phase, things had been going along swimmingly. Everything was in sync and all roads seemed to be leading to completion and delivery of the film to Universal Pictures. Carl was invited by and followed Keith into the restroom, and after a few minutes, Keith came out and sat back down at his spot next to Don Mitchell, the lead mixer. But Carl was nowhere to be seen. So I went into the restroom and there was Carl with a gleam in his eye and a smile and I must say, looking and feeling kind of celebratory, and a deer caught in the headlights. So we exit the restroom and Carl was fine and feeling happy because basically, his work was done. And then, pop, everything falls out of sync and Carl needs to get to the music reels and figure out what happened. But somehow, someway, Carl found he was able to throw everything back into sync and all's well that ends well as the Bard once said. I remember Keith saying to me that on this project, "He learned how to hear with his eyes." It was an incredibly powerful experience watching this movie unfold on a huge screen at the mixing stage and watching the collaboration between Taylor Hackford and Keith Richards.

Taylor, making sure that things worked dramatically on all levels cinematically and Keith making sure that the music held true to its musical intention with its integrity maintained. And here is that moment of confrontation which I alluded to earlier that I remember between Taylor and Keith; when Taylor, in the picture editing had added a "grand pause" in a song, as there was something that he wanted to capture in one of Chuck's expressions and make a dramatic point. But, that grand pause was not musically correct and Keith Richards objected. This turned into a bit of a serious confrontation outside the sound facilities stage, and in the end, with a determined Taylor Hackford protecting his vision and an equally passionate Keith Richards protecting the musical structure of one of the songs performed in St. Louis. In the end, Taylor prevailed and Keith acquiesced, but Keith had made his voice and feelings heard, loud and clear, and I can say that without hesitation.

In the end, *Hail! Hail! Rock 'N' Roll* did its job as a tribute to the legacy of Chuck Berry and all of the technical people and artists who were involved in bringing it to the screen were a part of making history, as Taylor Hackford once said. And as Keith Richards once said, "in the end, it will be here after we are all gone for future generations to come."

CHAPTER TWENTY
Chuck Arrested at Screening.

IN THE MOVIE'S AGREEMENT, *Chuck had final say on the film, and so a screening was arranged at Universal Studios for this purpose. Suzie Petersen, our executive from Universal, accompanied me to the screening. It would not go as planned, as was the usual case with our star, Chuck Berry. The film was produced on 35mm film so the viewing was in one of their large screening rooms with the projectionist and Chuck, myself and Suzie. Chuck walks in and immediately opens up a bag with a video camera inside, sets it up, and starts recording the film as it appears on the screen.*

STEPHANIE BENNETT: Do you remember the screening at Universal for Chuck Berry?

SUZIE PETERSEN: It is my best and clearest memory because it was at Universal. It was a massive freak out. Universal and all major studios were just incredibly protective of any kind of duplication of their film properties.

Initially the projectionist stopped the projection and came down to where we were sitting and told Chuck "you must stop filming or I have to call security." This didn't bother Chuck and he just continued.

SP: Even though it was Chuck, they still called the security people. And I knew they were going to. It was tense enough to have to watch the film and have to be worried about how Chuck was going to react to it and what he was going to say, and yet the whole furor became about his sitting there with his video camera and recording the film off the screen. Sure enough they sent security down, and security waited outside the door for us to come out. Our head of business affairs and legal affairs at the time had come down to try and head security off, and explain to them that it was Chuck and it was just a little video camera. It was certainly not that he was going to duplicate it in any way, but they didn't care. That was the rule so they took him over to the tower.

SB: I was freaking out, so I ended up calling the head of the studio Sean Daniels or Tom Pollock and said to them, "do you want the headline in tomorrow's paper saying "Chuck Berry arrested at Universal Studios."

SP: By this time Chuck was in the Tower with the security people. I think Chuck let them look at a few minutes and once they realized it was not a professional camera, they gave the tape back. Once you look back at the situation it became ridiculous, but at the time everyone in my group was freaking out not knowing what was going to happen and what that might mean for Chuck. It was like he was being arrested again as a black man doing something he wasn't supposed to do. It would have seemed horrible to him and he would have talked about it liberally.

The fact is he started off as a small-time crook. Went to jail for longer than perhaps a white person would have, and Taylor talks about how this created a kind of mentality or maybe he thought, "I am Chuck Berry and I can get away with it" (which he did). He was testing, always testing, and from what Dick Allen said he did that to everybody.

SP: Yes, the stories are legendary for that kind of stuff. There were so many levels of damage that racism had done, and yes, he was no angel, but is a textbook case of how bitter and angry he was, and rightfully so on many counts. Yeah, he was angry about it. I don't think he ever lost that feeling, "they are going to throw me into prison for some stupid thing again," because he didn't believe the things he did were any big deal.

I guess the only good thing to come out of it was that with all the goings-on around his filming the screening, he never had any comments or any changes and gave his approval to the film cut.

CHAPTER TWENTY-ONE
The Grand Publicity Tour

UNIVERSAL PICTURES WOULD TREAT the Chuck Berry film with a lot of promotion. Headed by Jane Ayer, the film would premiere in Los Angeles in Century City, the Ziegfeld in New York, and then on to London and Berlin and back to New York where we would receive the award by the National Board of Review for best documentary.

The premieres in Los Angeles and New York were carried out without much incident, and a party was held after the New York premiere, where I would find myself sitting between Keith and Chuck—my expression saying it all. And thinking, "phew, it's all over now, just London and Berlin and I never have to face this man again, who all but caused me a breakdown making the film." However, little did I know how wrong I was. Jane Ayer had worked with top music makers including, Ahmet Ertegun, but Chuck would be a challenge even for her.

JANE AYER: So we go to London for the premiere at Leicester Square. We were in first class. We arrive and check into the Royal Garden Hotel and then Chuck arrives pretty soon after. His book publisher's publicity person there, and all sorts of things were planned. She and I were liaising, but basically she took over. Also we found out he had planned a concert right after the premiere at the Hammersmith Palais.

I decided to have a nap knowing it would be a long night and I left a do not disturb on my phone. Next, there is a loud *knocking on the door and Jane is there, "Chuck won't come downstairs and meet the press." At this stage there were press and photographers from every newspaper in England. I get up and knock on his door and finally he answers. I asked him what the problem was and he tells me the publicity girl had indicated she was available and then rejected him. I said, "Chuck this is ridiculous. If you don't talk to the press they will publish her version of the story." Which is exactly what happened. He said, "well if they fire her I will come down." But he didn't, he took off.*

JA: The publicist was in tears and telling the press her story about Chuck making a pass at her. Meanwhile Chuck came down and took off in the concert promoter's Mercedes convertible and didn't show up for hours, until five minutes before his concert at the Hammersmith. The band he had to play with was panicking backstage wondering if he would show up. He showed up five minutes before, and just went on the stage and played. He had taken off in London driving on the wrong side of the road. I don't know where he went, what happened in all that time, but he came back and he played a great show. He gave everyone ulcers, except me maybe, I was the only one who said, "it's going to be fine." The exciting thing for me was we had this screening at the famous theater in Leicester Square. Then we had this after-party, some kind of chic club. There were two funny things that happened that I recall. Jeff Beck came up to me and asked me to introduce him to Chuck. It was like Christmas to Jeff. Then Chuck asked me to dance. Nobody was dancing. They were sort of waiting for him. I remember feeling really embarrassed. How could I dance with Chuck Berry and do the duck walk, but I did. The other thing he wanted was Indian food, separate from what they were serving there, so of course his wish was granted once again, we sat there with him while he ate.

I was furious at this point...he had done his usual "Nobody tells Chuck what to do or when." With no consideration for the people who were trying to promote his book and film, and of course he had to cram in another gig to make the trip worthwhile. I remember I couldn't wait for the next part of the trip to Berlin to be over.

JA: When we arrived in Berlin we got off the plane, and all I could think was there was a huge crowd and we got mobbed. It was like the footage of The Beatles when they were being mobbed during their heyday. And you and I were protecting Chuck from the crowd. It was unbelievable and we had to get security. We never thought we would need that. But he was such a force of nature and superstar in Berlin that it was pretty exciting to see that and scary at the same time.

The festival organized a screening and a press conference, which was mobbed. I remember I was still fuming and let Chuck answer the questions. I was so angry at his behavior in London. The only bright spot, though somewhat depressing to observe, was the Berlin Wall. Jane and I went to the wall and stood on steps looking over at the Russian soldiers.

JA: I remember flying to New York with Chuck and I had my British Passport. I hadn't become an American citizen yet, so I had to go through different customs. Chuck was really upset and worried, for some reason, I wouldn't get through or he didn't like that separation, but he was actually very kind about it, like he was concerned that something was wrong. But we got through and then went to the party in New York for directors.

STEPHANIE BENNETT: It was the National Film Review for documentaries. *Hail! Hail! Rock 'N' Roll* won the best film documentary award.

JA: I will never forget. I introduced Steven Spielberg to Chuck, and they were pleased to meet. Then I got this slap on my back, and I turn around and it's Donald Trump, and he wanted to meet Chuck Berry. He was so pushy about it.

SB: I sat next to him in the front row and he was with an attractive young woman and, in hardly a whisper, was talking to her about meeting him later. I didn't know his status at the time. Only later did I realize he was still married.

JA: It was absolutely the most memorable project or film I had worked on. I worked with a lot of people over the years. I worked with The Rolling Stones and Led Zeppelin, all of my music, you know Aretha Franklin, Elton John...major films at Universal, but this film had so many interesting connections and history and culture, and it really all came from Chuck. I mean the music...for me it was always the music. One of the things that I loved was when I was on the flight going with him and you from Berlin to New York. I was sitting next to him on that trip, and I talked to him about songwriting and for me that was the highlight, because my grandfather was the songwriter who wrote "Oh, You Beautiful Doll, If you Were the Only Girl In the World," these old Tin Pan Alley classic songs that he knew, and he started telling me about songwriting. I was mesmerized about that and how quickly he wrote the lyrics. I asked him about various songs, and he told me about how he wrote this song and this time, and he was so prolific and so important and really a cultural icon. But for me, I think the highlight of everything was that moment on that plane talking about songwriting, because it really is all about the song, and he was a master, along with everything else.

SB: Yeah, the storytelling in a song with the music.

JA: With a great melody, as simple and as hard as that is. But also working with Eric Clapton and Keith and you know all who have seen *Hail! Hail! Rock 'N' Roll* think there's a scene where Keith looks really tired and there's that whiskey bottle. It was three in the morning. He was exhausted. He was the hardest working person in show business that I had ever seen. He worked hard on that and put his heart and soul into it. You know Chuck didn't make it easy for him, for many people. I kind of, I was in a lucky spot, an easy spot. I didn't have that sort of tension, but I saw it all around me, you know, and you and Keith had it really tough.

SB: Yeah, it was like the ego, the egos, and the egos, but, and you know it's interesting, because the question is we never will know why he made it so difficult, why he was so resistant, why he didn't care. I think the problem was it was too late for him, because he had suffered so many years as a young man. When he took us into prison, it was like he was trying to give some payback, for the time when he could have been a young, black man enjoying. He had to hide Fran, his then girlfriend, who was with him when he died. He had to hide her under a blanket, because she was white. And so we forget that. When we took him to Jamaica to stay at Keith's he hated being called "bro." You know, The Stones got the groupies, Chuck got money, and that was his way of getting revenge, was money. Okay, I'll never be…Mick Jagger. I'll never be white, but I'll get money. They'll pay me. Payback. I will somehow get revenge. So it didn't matter who it was, as Dick Allen said, he did it to everybody. It was in his nature to seek some way of making sure he got his pound of flesh.

JA: And his garage full of Cadillacs.

SB: Everybody wanted to love him, but he wouldn't be loved. Wouldn't allow himself to be loved, or revered. He didn't care. I said to him, "you don't care about all these people being here." He said, "no." He told me that I don't care. How much? So it was like he was blinded to this whole thing that money equaled accolades. But it didn't. So even that show didn't. And that's what everybody was so frustrated about, that he didn't care. He didn't care.

CHAPTER TWENTY-TWO
Chuck's Passing

TAYLOR HACKFORD: Tom Adelman called me and told me. I was shocked and it was painful, because and as difficult as he was, I had a very good relationship with him. We did have a very cordial…even though he drove me crazy, we had a very cordial relationship. One day I met him for lunch. We laughed and we told stories, and it was not an adversarial situation with Chuck and me. I gave him a hug the last time I saw him, and he was like…it was an interesting thing. He was going to do *The Jay Leno Show*, which was taped live, but they do a sound check in the afternoon, so Chuck and I had lunch with Dick Allen and then I went in to see a sound check, which in typical fashion, he had a pickup band there, who were pretty good players and they were going to play, but it was an empty studio. It was probably three or four hours before the official taping when the audience would be let in and Jay Leno would be there and it would be a very live feeling to the show, and I looked around me and all of a sudden, people started to drift into this empty studio. They were NBC employees, there were people's secretaries and engineers from inside, various people who had heard that Chuck Berry was in the building and they were coming in to hear it, and I asked somebody, the stage manager, who was there, if that was normal. He said never, nobody comes in to see the sound check. They're coming in because they want to see a legend. They want in their lifetime to see Chuck Berry, and Chuck was completely oblivious to it. He got out there and he went through his things and the band played. But I recognized at that moment how special…I knew how special he was…that's why I did the film.

THOMAS ADELMAN: The first thing that I did when I heard that Chuck Berry had passed on March 18, 2017, one day before my birthday, was to reach out to Taylor Hackford to see if he had heard the news. He had not, and I remember his response, which was of course sad and reflective, and I knew that it must have been a moment frozen in time for Taylor. Taylor loved Chuck for what he had given to all of us musically and for what he had given to Taylor in the making of *Hail! Hail! Rock 'N' Roll*. When Stephanie and I talked about it, I knew that deep down inside, she was sad and feeling the pain on Chuck's passing. Chuck had taken a lot out of Stephanie Bennett in the making of this film, but he also gave her a lot, which ended up on the screen in the movie that she originally envisioned. Their relationship was complicated, but in the end, for Stephanie and all of us, it was all about getting it in the can, and giving something back to Chuck that would pay tribute to his legacy and stand the test of time for generations to come. This was certainly accomplished with the production of *Hail! Hail! Rock 'N' Roll*.

The passing of Chuck Berry represented the passing of an era which for many people reflected the soundtrack of their lives. Chuck Berry gave way to The Rolling Stones and The Beatles and many other British and American bands of that time that became the soundtrack for all of our lives. Chuck's musical footprint was like that of Neil Armstrong's footprint left on the lunar surface. Chuck was a discoverer, an explorer, and he came in musical peace for all mankind. Godspeed, Chuck Berry, and thank you.

STEPHANIE BENNETT: How did I feel? Well, I felt sad. The subject of my most challenging film had passed. And with his passing, a range of emotions surfaced within me. And some of those emotions were conflicting. Was this closure, was it not? Would I miss the dance? Chuck's death brought back the challenging adventure that making his film had confronted my team and I with. And yet, all these years later I am still proud of the movie that we made about Chuck. As you know by now, it wasn't easy, and Chuck kept me on my toes as a producer. Never knowing where or when the next tsunami was going to hit. I loved what he had contributed to the world as an artist. I didn't love the minefields that he had made Taylor and Keith and me and everybody walk through while we were trying to do something special for him. But I loved the experience and what we eventually were able to get onto the screen. Ultimately, through all the twisting and narrowing roads and passages that we had to maneuver through to get this film done, in the end it was worth it and I am glad that I did it. And I know that Chuck was proud of the movie and I also know that he knew what he had put me through. Chuck was a product of his times and he had to endure the trials and tribulations that being a black man, and a black artist at that, he was forced to confront on a daily basis in those early years. Those experiences made him who he was and clearly added an edge to his approach to dealing with the challenges that life tossed his way. As I have said, I have worked with many great artists on films, but the experience with Chuck was the most challenging and the scar tissue remains. I loved my compadres in arms, Taylor Hackford, Tom Adelman, Albert Spevak,

Jane Rose, and all of the others. And I loved the experience that we all shared. We are all still friends and this film will always be an experience that we all share, and one that I will forever be proud of. As Chuck said, "as long as they tell the truth, pro or con." Well, this is the truth. Farewell, Chuck Berry, and thank you for the dance.

CHAPTER TWENTY-THREE
Final Thoughts

TAYLOR HACKFORD: There's many things that I would have loved to have done. I would like to have dealt with Chuck's sex life. I would have loved to have dealt with his time in prison. And he's such a dark, incredible character, that every time you go into a situation with him, you're afraid its going to blow up in your face right and he's going to walk off and that's the end of the film, and so, you're walking on eggshells, and at the same time he's incapable of not doing something that's going to throw everybody out of control and at the same time have some spontaneity. But that's what I think is great about the film. So is it the film what I set out to make? No. I mean, there's a lot of things I planned that aren't in the film. But conversely, there's a lot of things in the film that weren't planned that are really wonderful and spontaneous, so like I said, it was a very unique experience and a great one for me. And when I look back, I go, "well, it isn't perfect, but it sure as hell was fun and interesting," and I think provocative and very revealing. You don't turn a camera on somebody and miss them. You know they think that they can shine on, the camera always reveals whoever they are. That's what I did. I said if I can get Chuck Berry and he'll actually reveal himself, whether he knows he's revealing himself or not, then collaborate with me. I saw the cars, I suggested he do that bit as the used car salesman. He loved it. He was brilliant. And that was a real, I would call that a creative dramatic collaboration between Chuck and I, using his cars. And he became the star and he was an actor then. He was fantastic, so there's a lot in that we could have never planned. It was again spontaneous. It was just a wild bronco ride, and a wild bronco ride is very, very exciting.

Chuck Berry was a very difficult subject, probably the most difficult that I've dealt with, but I loved him. And he gave a me a lot. Did he throw us some curves and did he renege on some promises? Maybe, kind of. But also he gave me a huge amount, and he did invite me into his life and he did show us a lot. And for that, I have huge gratitude for it. I love the guy. He was one of the more interesting people I met in my life. You know, Chuck Berry and Ray Charles, my God, two of the most important black people in American popular culture. And I had the opportunity of knowing them both personally. They both treated me extremely well. They may have mistreated people around me who worked on the films, but never with me, and it was a brilliant opportunity to collaborate with genius. I mean the true definition of genius, so, yeah, I'm thrilled with the film. I knew at the time it would be an historical record, and at this point I'm hoping that generations will have a change to really see this very complicated, dark human being. Complicated and incredibly talented.

And I think the film will stand the test of time.

TOM ADELMAN: I was the line producer of *Hail! Hail! Rock 'N' Roll.* Having been involved from the inception, it was a once in a lifetime journey, a magical mystery tour, and a snapshot in time, captured for all of us with this film and, now again, through this book. When I think back on those times, those things that stand out probably more than anything for me were the leadership and beautiful vision of Taylor Hackford for this film, and seeing his and Stephanie's dream come to life. The brilliant musical direction and courage of Keith Richards. And the courage, the unfliching courage, of Stephanie Bennett, who held this film together with spit and song and *Against All Odds*, as one of the Taylor Hackford movies was called. Stephanie had to tango through a minefield of strong personalities, all men, who were famous artists. Helen Mirren said that Taylor is a warrior, which he absolutely is. Well, Stephanie was a warrior, too, in my opinion, having stood by her and watched her prevail in a battle with Goliath.

STEPHANIE BENNETT: Being the only woman producer caught in a lion's den with Chuck Berry as the king of the jungle was a daunting challenge. And in those days, the glass ceiling, especially in Hollywood, was as high and impenetrable as a brick wall. But we prevailed and that glass ceiling suffered a few cracks. But, in the end, the only thing that really matters is that the film tells a story, as it happened, about a rock and roll hero caught in a trap, as Elvis Presley once said, tormented by inner demons, idolized by his contemporaries and a worldwide fan base. The film lifts the veil of his struggle with fame and being who he was. In the end, he really was Jonny B. Bad.

PHOTOS

—

Page 1: DVD cover of the movie *Hail! Hail! Rock 'N' Roll*.

Pages 2–3: Taylor Hackford filming at the Cosmopolitan Club in St. Louis, Missouri.

Pages 4–5: Author Stephanie Bennett with Keith Richards and Chuck Berry at a party.

Pages 6–7: Announcement of the show where Bruce Springsteen played back-up for Chuck Berry.

Pages 8–9: Bo Diddley, Little Richard, Chuck Berry, and Taylor Hackford.

Pages 10–11: Ticket for the first screening of the *Hail! Hail!*

Pages 10–11: Taylor Hackford (director) with Keith Richards, Chuck Levell, Johnnie Johnson, and Chuck Berry at the rehearsals at Berry Park.

Page 12: Keith Richards and Tom Adelman.

Page 12: Keith Richards and Chuck Berry in the car going to Keith's house in Jamaica.

Page 13: Keith Richards, Chuck Berry, Julian Lennon, Etta James, and Ingrid Berry (Chuck's daughter) together.

Page 13: Chuck Berry and Stephanie Bennett, first time in St. Louis.

Page 13: Algoa Prison where Chuck drove his car into the prison courtyard.

Page 13: Chuck Berry and Robbie Robertson looking at Chuck's scrapbook filmed for the movie.

Page 13: Chuck Berry.

Page 14: Chuck doing a show at the prison.

Page 14: Keith Richards and Chuck at Keith's house in Jamaica.

Page 14: Taylor Hackford filming Chuck at the Algoa Prison.

Page 15: Song selection from notes for the live performance at Fox Theatre, St. Louis.

Page 16: Taylor Hackford and Helen Mirren on the set of the movie *White Nights*.

ACKNOWLEDGMENTS AND THANKS

Taylor Hackford

Universal Pictures

Jim Mervis

Murray Weiss

Joel Gotler

Barbara Ligerti

Karen Hitzig

Helen Mirren

Dick Allen

Scott Richardson

Robbie Robertson

Jared Levine

Keith Richards

Jane Rose

Joey Spampinato

Little Richard

Johnnie Johnson

Bo Diddely

Bruce Springsteen

Bob Gruen

Jane Ayer

Suzie Petersen

Steve Jordan

Oliver Stapleton

Suzie Petersen

Albert Spevak

Carl Colpaert

Heidi Crane